50 Worst Dates

Jane Laboucane

This book reflects the author's recollections of experiences over time. The author has tried to represent the events as faithfully as possible. All names have been changed to protect the privacy of individuals.

First paperback edition September 2023

Cover design by Bailey McGinn

ISBN: 978-1-7390491-0-2

To all those who have had a terrible time with men—may your dates be better than mine.

CONTENTS

INTRODUCTION

This book is a collection of stories about dates I've gone on in my quest to find "The One." The stories are all true and are told according to my recollection; any mistakes are purely due to a faulty memory on my part. Names have been changed to protect peoples' privacy and some locations have been omitted. Each chapter is, mostly, independent of the next, but there are two people who pop up repeatedly throughout the text: Babycakes and Mr. Situationship, Brent. Babycakes was my long-term boyfriend of nearly a decade. He works in finance and some of his clients have included past presidents, owners of professional sports teams, and high-flyers in the fashion and entertainment industry. Our relationship was a dumpster fire of breakups and make-ups, and our dates take up nearly half of this book. Brent, a.k.a. Mr. Situationship, recurs in the latter part of this book. Our Situationship spanned nearly two years and was the definition of dysfunction. The remaining twenty-four dates cover everything from one-offs to partnerships that lasted for a few months.

BABYCAKES 1

We met at an interesting time in both our lives. He was recently separated from his wife (it turns out that they were going to counselling and still living together—he was just seeking out fun and dating around in cities that weren't his own) and I was just starting university in Toronto. When I met him, he had a vodka addiction, which he reverentially referred to as "vodka demons." The early stages of our relationship revolved around going out to fancy restaurants for dinner, followed by bar-hopping and getting rip-roaringly drunk. It was common for us to go back to our hotel room and for me to have to build him a pillow-fort next to the toilet. I will tell you this—you've never had a pillow-fort until you've had one at the Ritz. Sometimes he would crawl into bed in the middle of the night, but other times I would wake up the next morning and find him curled up in the fetal position around the toilet, his head resting on a vomit-stained pillow. I would pat him on the arm to make sure he was still alive, and he would groan in deep hangover pain and despair. I would throw a blanket over him and dial up room service for some sustenance, which sometimes included Clamato juice to make 6 a.m. Caesars.

We all have our demons.

THAT TIME I DATED A GRANDPA

I met him on Bumble. Gerald was a wine drinker. I can relate, but he and I had one thing that set us apart. There are two kinds of winos in this world: the ones who appreciate the taste and love a good bottle of wine, and those who buy it by the box—Costco-sized. Both types of winos can routinely overindulge, but those who buy it by the box are a different breed. They are flat-out drinking to get drunk. I, too, am sometimes drinking to get drunk, but I have a palate that I like to think is one small step up from cardboard.

I digress.

True to form, Gerald took me to a super-secret wine club one evening. A black Escalade picked us up and whisked us off to a non-descript, east-end building. I had not been apprised of what we were doing that evening, much less where we were going, and I was a bit confused when we walked through a set of glass doors into a corporate building. The lobby looked like that of most typical skyscrapers, with minimal but tasteful décor. Nothing loud and obnoxious, nothing too comfortable or cold. It was an empty space—I don't even recall seeing a security guard in the vicinity, although I'm sure there was one.

Gerald guided me to the right, just past the glass doors, where a large, metal wall stood tall, and pointed to a piece of technology that discretely jutted out from the wall. He placed his thumb on the pad, where a laser scanned it, and the metal wall suddenly revealed itself to be a metal door.

It was some James Bond, badass shit that I had never seen before, nor have I seen since. He guided me inside, where there was a set of stairs that led into a darkly lit cavern with squishy furniture, wood-tones, and hazy lights. People were scattered about the cave, which had a wrought iron cage holding several rows of drawers off to one side. We were, Gerald explained, at a wine club. This made sense because Gerald was, after all, a wino. What *didn't* make sense was that we were at a very high-end, exclusive wine club that ostensibly housed vintages worth thousands of dollars, while Gerald drank wine exclusively from a box. I waited with bated breath for him to show me to his wine drawer. What would it hold? I pictured the finest, Costco-sized boxed wine available for purchase and wondered what would set it apart from the rest. Would the plastic tap come sealed with red wax? Would the box look aged like it had been on a round-the-world tour with FedEx, or have nibbled-off corners in a testament to how long it had fermented underground? Would it taste like actual wine and not give off the grimace-inducing aftertaste that denotes shit from a box? Sadly, I didn't get a chance to see. Instead of raiding his own stock, we sat at one of the bars and shared a bottle from one of his friends. I didn't know if this was to preserve the Costco stash, or if Gerald only brought his out on special occasions. After all, once the box has been opened, that's several gallons one must drink to avoid wasting wine.

A few days later, we went to his industrial-area office when, on our way to a few (surprise) wineries, and I saw a smattering of children's toys scattered around the floor. It occurred to me that it was rather strange for a construction company—a place where heavy equipment, sharp tools, and dust and dirt accumulated—to play host to children. So, I asked Gerald about it.

"Oh," he said nonchalantly. "Those are for my daughter's children."

Daughter's children? It took me a second to grasp what this meant…and then it hit me like a dump truck—I was dating a grandpa.

I processed this information as we climbed into his Cadillac convertible and left the building. We drove around backroads, hitting up different wineries where I proceeded to drink myself into oblivion. It was a beautiful autumn day, but I found it hard to focus on the scenery or anything other than the wine. We stopped at four wineries and then a bar, for good measure, before we headed back into the city.

I had realized at the first winery that drinking my face off would not erase the memory of my paramour being a grandfather but would just result in me being shit-faced and massively hungover the next day.

Still, I persisted.

True to form, my premonition came true and I realized in the midst of an unholy hangover the next day that I had to end it. I simply could not be a thirty-year-old step-grandmother living out my days drinking boxed wine from Costco.

Gerald was good about it, and I have only fond memories of him that come rushing back every time I end up in the cheap-wine section of my local liquor store.

BABYCAKES 2

Prior to meeting Babycakes, I had never understood the green-faced emoji that denotes sickness. *Why green?*, I would question. Green isn't even a skin colour. I have seen people go white with terror, pale with sickness, red with anger, fuchsia with embarrassment, but never green—not until Babycakes and I went out on our first date.

We met at a French restaurant for drinks and Babycakes wore his attentive, salesman façade. He asked all the right questions, seemed rapt with interest, and was a total gentleman. We had only agreed to go for a couple of drinks, but I didn't know that Babycakes had other ideas. He was a man on a mission, and he had planned on making a night of it. After lulling me into a false sense of security, he gently suggested dinner. I was enjoying his company so I agreed and we made our way over to one of the city's best fine-dining establishments. It was a quaint space, situated in a brick building, and Babycakes pulled out all the stops. He ordered an over-the-top expensive bottle of wine in an attempt to impress me, which was a failure on two counts:

One, I was young and would drink anything if I liked the taste; Two, I knew next to nothing about wine. I grew up in a family where my grandfather routinely made the moonshine equivalent. A good bottle of fermented grapes was measured by its potency and not its cost or the taste. Could it get you shit-faced? Yes? That's a good batch.

After dinner, we walked over to a patio—it was a warm night and we had more drinks while deciding what to do. Babycakes was a conservative type, so I suggested that we go to a gay bar. By this point I could tell that he wanted in my pants, and I wanted to know just to what lengths he would go to get there.

He agreed to go to the gay bar, and I dragged him up to the third floor where most of the men in attendance were dancing, sweaty and shirtless, to Britney. Babycakes was wearing a black tailored suit and a poorly-concealed look of horror. He met one of my friends who was bartending that night, and I dragged Babycakes onto the dance floor where I kissed him amidst a sweaty crowd of shirtless guys.

By the time we left, I was definitely tipsy and decided that we needed a 2 a.m. snack. Babycakes, in his quest to get laid, was up for anything. Part-way through my French fries I declared that I was sleeping over. Babycakes, in a tactic he taught me when it comes to negotiations and sales, shut up and smiled. In business, he later explained (and in the business of getting someone into bed), once you've obtained your target, you keep your mouth closed.

It had been a boozy eight hours that we had spent together and, when I woke up the next morning, I was certainly feeling it. When Babycakes rolled over, I could tell that he was feeling it, too. I have seen and experienced a lot of hangovers in my life but this was the only time I have ever seen someone so sick that they turned a rotten hue of honeydew. I left him that morning, his skin a putrid shade of green that made me sick just looking at him.

I thought that I would never see him again. Instead, it turned into a decade-long affair that was equal parts love, hate, and liquor.

THE KLEPTOMANIAC CELEBRITY CHEF

He was the epitome of tall, dark, and handsome and yet another Bumble discovery. He was also of the blue checkmark variety because of his status as a celebrity chef. On our first date, we walked down to the waterfront, shared a bottle of wine on a patch of grass, and talked until long after the sun went down. He had a great sense of humor and, in addition to being handsome, he was just enough of a weirdo to have me hooked.

We spent the next couple of weeks hanging out together at various haunts around the city. One Thursday night I took him to gay karaoke where I proceeded to get absolutely annihilated on vodka. We sang duets on stage and the evening ended with me kicking him out of the cab on the way home because he didn't want to sleep with me. We hadn't had sex yet, and in my inebriated state I was offended that he wasn't chomping at the bit to get me into bed. Turns out he just wanted to wait (a novel concept that I had not encountered with anyone before nor since). We ended up doing the deed a short time later and everything seemed to be going well. As we grew closer, we both started opening up to each other. One afternoon, this took a turn for the worse.

We had spent a cozy autumn day on a patio, wrapped in a warm fleece blanket provided by the restaurant. After several drinks and some light snacks, we decided that it was time to go. The weather had turned chilly and it was a long walk home, so he pilfered the blanket and wrapped it around me for our stroll back to my place. We were walking along in companionable silence when he suddenly spoke.

"You know . . . I like to steal things," he said.

I looked at him sideways.

"Like, drunkenly?" I inquired. After all, who among us has not gotten the urge to stuff a salt shaker into their purse after a few too many cocktails? Just me? Okay then.

"No," he said with a slight smirk. "When I go to the grocery store and other places."

I was taken aback at this and asked for clarification despite it being quite clear that he had just told me that he likes to steal from stores. Sober.

"I feel entitled to it," he mused. "I'll just slip things into my pockets or inside of my coat. And if I ever get caught, I'm tall and handsome and I know I will be able to talk my way out of it."

This was disturbing to me. My mother drunkenly stealing a candle from a bar on a crazy, Captain Morgan-fueled night out? Acceptable. My boyfriend soberly stealing an expensive bottle of olive oil on a Tuesday afternoon at a grocer? Unacceptable. I felt wary after this and made him promise me that he wouldn't steal anything when I was around.

Of course, kleptomania is a red flag—a *massive* red flag. But I really liked him, thus illustrating my other problem when it comes to dating, aside from choosing poorly. Once

I've decided that I like someone, I *really* like them. Having to ask a partner not to steal things when they are with you is a problem. But I continued dating him until he ghosted me. I have seen him around, though, on one particular dating app, where he has swiped right on me no fewer than five times. I did not pay the right-swipe back. Steal my heart once, shame on you. Steal my heart twice, shame on me. And just soberly steal anything in general, shame on him.

BABYCAKES 3

Most people I have encountered, when they hear a fire alarm sound, unless they are in an office that forces them to leave the building, tend to sit back, relax, and wait for the all-clear to continue on with what they are doing. Only on rare occasions do people abandon their belongings and flee the building.

The hotel that Babycakes and I were staying at had been undergoing some renovations. To that end, fire alarms, we were warned by the front-desk staff, were a common occurrence. We had been there for two nights but had yet to experience any.

That changed, however, at 3 a.m. on a Thursday.

I'm a light sleeper, but Babycakes is the lightest sleeper I have ever encountered. I suppose it would have served him well in the caveman days when it paid to be on high alert for predators, but in present day, it was a bit annoying. I reach over to the nightstand to grab a glass of water in the middle of the night? He jolts out of a deep, snore-filled sleep, sits up and yells "What's going on?"

In this instance, Babycakes was sleeping the alcohol-fueled sleep of the truly hammered. It was winter and his penchant for a particular piano bar that catered to his lust for liquor and inability to control his intake had factored into the evening. To that end, while I loved the piano bar, the music, and the staff who worked there, I was always weary any time he suggested we go there, which was, typically, every evening. It's 9 p.m. on a Tuesday and we've just finished post-dinner cocktails? Piano bar. It's 5 p.m. on a Monday and we've just finished afternoon cocktails? Piano bar.

You see where I'm going with this.

When sitting around the piano bar, the staff, who knew Babycakes' go-to beverage, also knew at approximately what intervals to serve him to keep him in a steady state of inebriation.

It had been an evening full of several vodkas and the man could have been hit by a Mac truck and he wouldn't have felt any pain. We cabbed it back to the hotel, went up to our 26th floor room and both fell into a deep slumber. Babycakes was snoring in a manner that, I have discovered, is only attainable by men and large-breed dogs. You know the kind. The kind where you simultaneously want to punch them in the face and smother them with your pillow. The alcohol had him in a deep sleep, but suddenly, a shrill ringing began blasting from the speaker above our bed. I jolted awake in confusion and looked at the clock—it was just after 3 a.m. At the same time, I felt the covers beside me fly off of the erstwhile occupant, who had launched himself out of bed in a flurry of curse words.

"Jesus-motherfucking-goddamned-fucking-christ, cock sucker, motherfucker. . ." he angrily spat out, continuing his curse-laden tirade without pause. I lay there, listening to his obscenities and the ringing alarm, while trying to make sense of his behaviour. In addition to cursing like a trucker, Babycakes was putting on his dress pants, dress shirt, suit jacket, and was searching for his socks. I observed for a bit but finally, laughter in my voice, asked: "What the fuck are you doing?"

"Getting dressed," he said aggressively. "I don't want to get fucking burned up. I'm going to take the stairs to the fucking lobby. Fucking 3 a.m. fire alarm. Piece of shit fucking hotel."

This was bizarre. Babycakes, who at this point, still had a blood alcohol content of four times the legal limit, was putting on his suit and was planning to leg it down 26 flights of stairs at 3 a.m. to avoid death by fire. I pointed out to him that he was more likely to die from drunkenly falling down the stairs, but he was unconvinced. I did, however, with some calmed reasoning, manage to get him to lay on top of the covers with his suit on to wait for an update from the fire department.

"Fine," he said aggressively. "I'll stay here for 10 minutes. But if I die in a fire, it's your fault."

As expected, the fire department came through our speaker and told us to remain in our room for further instruction, and tens of minutes later, they told us it had been a false alarm. Like it is 99.9999% of the time.

Now, I'm not dismissing fire safety and taking fire alarms seriously. I am, however, questioning the judgement of an individual who is afraid he's going to die in a fire but who has no safety concerns when it comes to taking 26 flights of stairs with a B.A.C of 4 while sleep deprived. His selective concern for self-preservation was fascinating. I mean, in a fire at least he was so alcohol-soaked that it would be a quick death. The human equivalent of a Roman candle.

CONFESSIONS

Mark's Bumble profile immediately spoke to me. Blond, blue-eyed, above six-feet tall and a mischievous and enticing smile. I scrolled down his profile and read his "About Me" with interest. When I arrived at the "We will get on if" part of it, I was sold. What was he looking for in a partner? What was a surefire way to ensure compatibility? Was it a dedication to fitness? A love of intellectual conversation? An appreciation for his golden retriever?

No.

It was none of the above.

Mark had concluded that you would be compatible with him if, and I quote: "You enjoy Michelin restaurants but are also genuinely concerned you'll blackout before we get the cheque."

This man spoke to my soul. Though I do a bang-up job of presenting like a lady, I am, for all intents and purposes, a massive shit-show at times. I like to have fun. And what I mean by that is that I like to have the most fun I can at any given moment. This oftentimes involves massive amounts of liquor.

Mark and I exchanged a flurry of messages, determining on the first day of texting that we were a suitable match. During texting Day Two was when our relationship really began to be challenged. He messaged me *Good morning,* which somehow turned into a conversation about university.

I should tell you, he wrote. *I was charged with a Class 2 felony.*

My eyebrows raised to my hairline. *Oh?* I replied.

Yes. I started using drugs in university and then started selling them to pay for my habit.

I paused and Googled "Class 2 Felony drugs," and another message popped up on my screen.

I was facing fifteen years in prison but was able to get off with probation. But unfortunately, it disqualified me from pharmacy and medical school, so now I'm in sales.

Given that he had previously been facing fifteen years in prison for selling drugs, I figured that the man had definitely found his career calling.

One thing I have found as I've gotten older—and the dating pool has begun to drain—is that things like Class 2 felonies and almost spending fifteen years in prison are seen as a minor blip. Sure, he lives with his parents and delivers pizzas part-time, but he's saving for an apartment and paying off his debt. At least he *has* a job. And Mark, my almost-felon, was more than a part-time pizza delivery driver—he was gainfully *and* successfully employed.

Our conversation continued.

On Tuesday, he confessed that he had broken up with his long-term girlfriend six months earlier and that he had only been on one date during that time. This was promising—he had yet to experience the bad dating that comes from apps.

We continued texting.

On Wednesday, he told me he was moving out of his current condo. *I should tell you something,* he wrote. *I am moving into a new place tomorrow because I have been living with my ex-girlfriend for the past six months.*

Sleeping in the same bed?

We only have one, he wrote back.

I pondered this but continued texting.

On Thursday, the conversation turned to regular drug use. Perhaps deriving inspiration from his confession a few days earlier about his almost-felony. *I drink heavily pretty often and I have an addictive personality,* he typed. *But I've learned to rein it in. I have to confess to you, though. I smoke pot every day.*

Now, I'm hardly a prude, but if you're ingesting any kind of mind-altering substance every day, it's probably not in the best interest of your health.

Like, once a day? I replied. I could maybe deal with once per day—drained dating pool and whatnot.

Multiple times per day, he responded, adding on that this included the stoner special that's known as a "Wake and Bake." *I hope that's not going to scare you off,* he wrote.

At this, I laughed. The man had confessed to me that he was an almost felon, he was still currently living and sleeping with his ex-girlfriend in the same bed, and that he drinks heavily and often, but he wanted to make sure that him smoking pot every day wasn't going to scare me off?

At this point, I sat back, tallied up the confessions, and decided that while I could live with a convict who smoked pot multiple times per day, every day, drank heavily, was very fresh to the dating scene and who was currently sleeping in the same bed as his ex-girlfriend, he had confessed one confession too many. This was only Day Five of us texting and there had already been five revelations. I couldn't live like that—always waiting for the next "I should tell you something" text or "I have to confess" conversation. I chose to cut my losses, unmatched, and moved on.

BABYCAKES 4

One thing I loved about Babycakes was his utter and complete lack of shame. There is something endearing about a person who literally could not give any fucks about what others think of them and who is immune to embarrassment. That's the kind of confidence I dream of. And that's the kind of confidence I want in a man. The kind where he could shit his pants in public and, pun intended, not give two shits about it.

I mean this literally.

You may recall me mentioning it previously, but Babycakes has a bit of an alcohol addiction. On one particular night, we were staying at the Ritz-Carlton, which has a large, open lobby that contains two ground-floor lounges. Babycakes had not been feeling well that week and was on antibiotics. Of course, this did not stop him from drinking. Not at all. What it did do, though, was give him a seriously upset stomach. After walking through the front doors of the hotel into the lobby after a night out, he felt concerning rumblings in his stomach. Knowing that there was a bathroom directly across from the front desk,

Babycakes strode purposefully in that direction. He didn't make it in time, however, and, dressed in one of his four-thousand-dollar Zegna suits, he shit his pants. Right there. In the lobby of the Ritz-Carlton.

Shuffling to the bathroom, he proceeded into a stall where he took off his pants, removed his underwear, and threw them into the garbage. After putting his pants back on and washing his hands, he exited the bathroom and walked back into the lobby. And what did he do at this point? Did he go directly to the elevators and back to his room to contemplate what had just happened and be near a bathroom in case it happened again?

He did not.

Instead, he went to one of the lobby lounges to order himself a drink for the road. Now, I don't know about you, but if I had shit my pants in a hotel lobby and had to throw out my underwear, I would go directly to my room out of fear of that happening again. I would be mortified and, even though no one else was any the wiser, I would decide that I could never stay at that hotel again because of the bad memories it would bring. I would never be able to set foot in that Ritz-Carlton without reliving the horror of me shitting my pants.

Babycakes? Not so much. It was merely an inconvenience in his quest for liquor. He wouldn't let a little thing like uncontrollable diarrhea and having to throw out his underwear stop him from reaching his goal.

Drink in hand, he made it to the elevator bank where he stood, swaying to-and-fro while waiting for one of the three elevators to take him to his floor. It was at this point where his stomach betrayed him again and, with no underwear acting as a barrier, he proceeded to shit on the floor, literally shaking it out of his pant leg as a group of people rounded the corner. At the Ritz.

He did not, as I would have done, die of shame. He did not, as I would have done, avoid that hotel like the plague. He laughed about it and continues to laugh about it to this day, and he still stays at that hotel. I am convinced that the hotel staff have video of this incident and that it has been widely shared amongst friends and family. Babycakes doesn't mind. He still finds it funny.

THE DEARLY DEPORTED

We met on Bumble. His profile photo showed him wearing a black suit and a happy smile; his name was Alan. Like my right-swipes before him, what drew me towards him, looks aside, was his "We will get on if" statement, which read, "We will get on if: you enjoy getting drunk and stealing things."

Boom! That's a match.

Alan was staying at the upscale, downtown hotel that had played into so much of my life. He was in the city, raising investment funds for his gold mine. Yes. He *owned* a gold mine.

I had arranged two dates for that evening and as soon as I showed up to the first one, I knew it wasn't going anywhere. My date was nice, but he wasn't my type. Mostly, I couldn't wait to see Alan, my Date Number Two. We had exchanged a couple of messages that day and it appeared that we would get on. He was a bit shorter than I preferred, but good conversation can mean a lot.

I took the elevator to the top-floor restaurant and met him at the bar. Square, black-rimmed glasses framed his face and were complemented by a black suit jacket and jeans. Immediately, I was hooked. We chatted and bantered late into the evening before heading to a pub down the street. My stomach hurt from laughing and my face was sore from smiling by the time we parted outside the pub several hours later.

We spent the next several days together, engaging in low-key adventures all over Toronto, never running out of things to talk or laugh about. And the day before he was slated to leave, he extended his trip by one week so that we could spend more time together. We continued on with more of the same.

On Alan's last day in the city, we met at a sports bar near his hotel. He was taking a midnight flight and we planned to spend the day together before he jetted off overseas. We drank sangria and talked for about an hour before he picked up something from the chair beside him and handed it to me. It was a blue, moleskin journal and a card. "J," it read, "By far the best part of this trip has been meeting you. Thanks for showing me around and for all of the belly laughs. You're lovely. Much love, Alan." It was one of the sweetest gifts I had ever received, and I kept the card on my fridge for months. When he left later that evening, getting into an Uber at the hotel, I felt an overwhelming sense of sadness. He would come back, he promised—hopefully in six months. I hoped, but I kept my expectations low and tried to appreciate our two-week encounter for what it was. If we kept in touch, he came back, and something actually came from it, then that would be great. But if none of that happened, that would be okay, too. He did, after all, live on the other side of the world.

We did end up keeping in touch—texting on a daily

basis, video-chatting, and talking on the phone. He sent photos, I sent photos, and we grew closer—both of us having cute nicknames for each other. He sweetly referred to me as "Blue Jay," a nickname that was the catalyst for something that later led me to the first indication that something with Alan may not have been quite right. One day, four weeks after he had left, he sent me a picture of his bare arm. Only, his arm wasn't quite bare—he had a very, *very* large bird tattoo on his bicep. A blue jay. Nice artwork to be sure, but there is something about tattooing something so large in dedication to someone whom you barely know on your body that is unsettling. Some might see it as romantic, but I viewed it as impulsive.

"It's fine," he reassured me. "If things don't work out, at least I will always have this as a memory for the incredible time that we spent getting to know each other."

When he framed it that way, it didn't sound so bad. But still. It was a massive bird.

One week later, there was another indication that something about Alan wasn't quite right. He sent me some videos he had taken in New Zealand. One consisted of him telling me how he had nearly been arrested at the airport because he had gotten into a fight with the staff. He managed to talk his way out of it and assured me he was going to apologize to the employees on his way back.

Now, I fully understand impatience and how stressful time spent at the airport can be—especially if there are things such as flight delays and lost luggage. But I also realize that a rational adult does not typically fly off the handle, berate airline staff, and nearly get arrested.

Still, I persisted—albeit with a bit more caution. By this time, Alan had already booked a flight back to see me and secured a condo close to mine for a three-month stint. I was looking forward to seeing him and brushed any apprehension I felt to the back of my mind.

In the time leading up to his return, he told me stories about going out with hotel staff until 4 a.m. at places that he was staying and enduring raging hangovers that were only abated by the addition of weed. Later, he told me about how he had taken Ambien while at home one evening because of his unrelenting insomnia and had woken up to discover the paintings in his house had been defaced. He later realized that the culprit was not a crazed, art aficionado who had broken into his house to deface his paintings, but that he himself, in his Ambien state-of-mind, had secured a paintbrush and gone to town.

My unease grew. Still, he was coming back to my country and I was looking forward to seeing him. Plus, I knew that he had a very stressful job and that sometimes stress can manifest in different ways.

The Saturday that he was slated to arrive I received a phone call around 4 p.m. This, I knew, was Alan. He was at the condo and was waiting for me.

I was half right.

It was Alan, yes, but he was *not* at the condo, nor was he waiting for me. He was actually in a hospital on the other side of the country.

It turned out that Alan had decided to take a few Xanax during his overseas flight so that he would be refreshed when he arrived to see me. Part-way through the flight, however, he decided that it would be a good idea to take a few more. With liquor. He had taken six Xanax in all with Jesus knows how many drinks and, when the plane arrived on the West Coast, the flight attendants could not wake him. Once they finally roused him, Alan was, apparently, in the mood for a fight.

"What's your address?" he asked me, sounding groggy. He needed it to give to border security and he would have to show proof of prescription for the Xanax once he reached customs.

Alarmed, I provided him with my address, wished him well, asked him to call when he arrived, and hung up the phone. This was concerning. Not just Alan being in the hospital, but him thinking nothing of popping six Xanax and drinking himself into oblivion on a trans-Pacific flight. It struck me as particularly poor judgment.

Regardless, I sat and waited. I read a book to keep from pacing my condo. Six hours later, I received a phone call from Alan. He had arrived in my city and been detained by border agents. After being unable to provide proof of prescription for the Xanax, the border agents booked him on the next flight back to Sydney. He tearfully apologized and promised he would have his lawyer get him back into my country.

You could have hit me in the face with a frying pan at that moment, and I merely would have stood there and stared. I was so shocked at how things had unfolded that I was completely nonplussed. I had been prepared for Alan to lose his passport and I had been prepared for Alan to board the wrong plane. I had not been prepared for him to be deported. It was not, however, without irony. Numerous times, in the heat of rage, I have plotted ways to get a foreigner ex-boyfriend, who had recently dumped me, deported. And now, a boyfriend had gone and deported himself.

The humor was not lost on me.

Alan made it back to Sydney unscathed except, he claimed, for a broken heart. While there he holed up in a downtown hotel room. Our last contact came several hours after he had messaged me to tell me that he was going fully sober—giving up drugs, drinks, and prescription meds. Three hours later I received a text message and accompanying picture that showed him in a bar, getting a psychic reading.

That was the moment I stepped off the crazy train. I will put up with a lot, but this was too much, even for me. Some Googling six months later confirmed that the crazy train had indeed derailed when I read that Alan had been removed as president of his company. He didn't do much damage to me, miraculously, but I'm not sure if his shareholders got off quite as unscathed.

BABYCAKES 5

One thing Babycakes really got me into was March Madness—the NCAA college basketball tournament. Universities from across America compete in a tournament that is full of upsets and great basketball games. This particular night was during the middle of the tournament.

We were sitting at a sports bar in the downtown Toronto core and had dinner reservations for later that evening. The dinner reservation was for one of my favorite places, but it was early enough in the afternoon that we needed a snack to soak up all the beer we were drinking. This particular sports bar, unbeknownst to us, had massive portions. We ordered flatbread and nachos. What the bartender placed in front of us were two platters that were enough to feed ten people—the two of us didn't even make a dent.

Living in an area where there are a lot of homeless people around, I wanted to make sure that the untouched flatbread and essentially untouched nachos were given to someone in need instead of being thrown into the trash.

To that end, we had the snacks packed up and we left the bar, with Babycakes sporting a frown because the team he had bet on had lost. The restaurant where we had reservations was only a five-block walk away, and I figured that there would be someone to whom we could offer a meal along the way.

I was wrong.

This was the only time in my history of living in that city that I walked five blocks and didn't see a needy person in sight. But I was determined. I had had the food packaged up specifically because I wanted to give it to someone in need. Now, I just needed to find that someone. Babycakes, meanwhile, just wanted to go to the restaurant.

I insisted that we keep walking.

After twenty minutes and hitting up nearly the entire downtown core, I was feeling defeated. I had never before and have never since encountered that area so void of impoverished people. This should be seen as a positive—if there are no people sleeping on the street, that means that they are all being taken care of. But in that moment, I couldn't see it that way. I was being selfish. I wanted to do a good deed, but the impoverished people were not cooperating.

We kept walking.

At one point, Babycakes pointed out that because we had put on so many miles, he was someone in need—of a drink—and if it would make me happy, he would eat the flatbread and nachos. I asked for ten more minutes. By this point, Babycakes, who typically has very little patience to begin with, was starting to get annoyed. I could see his blood pressure rising with each empty street corner. I finally gave up when it became clear that someone in need of a meal was not going to magically appear on the sidewalk.

As we proceeded to the restaurant, an angry Babycakes fumed beside me. His basketball team had lost, which meant that he had lost money on his bet; he was looking forward to a nice dinner and instead he had spent thirty minutes being dragged around every corner downtown in the bitter cold.

We finally arrived at the restaurant, and the waiter brought us to our table. It was a great table—up against a wall where we could see the entire restaurant but were a bit hidden away. Babycakes was finally starting to relax, and the waiter came over to take his drink order. He is very particular about his libations. He likes a double vodka in a tumbler, with a twist of lemon and one ice cube. The waiter walked away to get our drinks, at which point Babycakes and I began to argue. About what, I don't remember, but it was likely due to: him being hungry, me being pissed off over my charity fail, him losing a sports wager, and me being annoyed that he was annoyed. The waiter came back just as the eye-rolling and exasperated "Oh my Gods" commenced, and he set Babycakes' drink down in front of him.

The drink was not a double vodka in a tumbler with a twist of lemon and one ice cube. Instead, it was vodka in a martini glass with no ice and a lemon slice.

The waiter put my beer down in front of me and walked away while Babycakes and I sat there, staring at his martini. I could tell that this was the straw that was going to break the camel's back. I just didn't know what Babycakes was going to do. Was he going to stand up and flip the table? Was he going to walk over to the waiter and give him a piece of his mind? Was he going to unleash a torrent of curse words and smack his glass to the ground?

He did none of the above.

Instead, he gazed far off into the distance with a "Fuck

my life" look in his eyes and started singing in a monotone voice: *"Take me home, country roads, to the place, I belong, West Virginia, mountain mama, take me home, country roads."*

John Denver had never sounded so pitiful. And I had never been so confused. I was prepared for yelling, I was prepared for swearing, I was prepared for table flipping, I was prepared for embarrassment. I was not prepared for a woefully sad version of "Country Roads" sung by an inebriated fifty-year-old in an upscale restaurant. People were staring.

"It calms me down," he explained, his voice still monotone, his eyes still gazing off into the distance in search of some salvation.

I laughed my ass off.

The waiter did come back and rectify Babycakes' drink order, and I learned an entertaining lesson that evening: When things go south and Babycakes looks like he's going to explode, put on John Denver.

1 + 3 = A CALCULATION SO CONFUSING THAT I REQUIRE THE AID OF FRIENDS AND FAMILY

I met him on a dating app and he looked vaguely like Donny Osmond—if Donny Osmond sported box-dyed black hair and walked with a limp. He was a prominent ex-lawyer who was known in the legal world as a "fixer." Essentially, he would go into companies to root out problems and the people who were causing them and "fix" it through legal maneuverings and employee firings. There was something deliciously attractive about it, and he told me stories about ordering employees into his office and giving them a low-voiced, deliberate dressing down before compiling enough information to legally terminate their employment. He wielded his power with impunity and meted out punishments with glee—it was very villain-esque. And I have always had a thing for villains. Screw James Bond in all of his Daniel Craig hotness—give me the bad guys in *Skyfall*, *Casino Royale*, and *Spectre*.

For our first date, we went out for wine on a popular uptown patio. The conversation flowed along with the alcohol, and we went our separate ways. A few days later, on Saturday morning, he texted me to ask if I wanted to drive up to his friend's house in an area outside of the city. His friend, Collin, was there with his girlfriend, Ally. I agreed and he suggested that I pack an overnight bag just in case.

The drive down was pleasant—it was a beautiful summer afternoon and we cranked Boston and Lynyrd Skynyrd as we high-tailed it out of the city in his Mercedes. Collin, I was given to understand, was in his late sixties and owned a penthouse in a storied hotel. After turning off the highway, we drove down paved back-roads, taking in the foliage while we navigated our way to his friend's estate. We were greeted by Collin as we pulled into the driveway—he had a shaggy mop of hair swept casually over his face, and he gave off the air of a yogi. Shortly after, he ushered us into the kitchen where Ally, his girlfriend, sat: all twenty-two years old of her.

But I liked her.

Far from being the plastic, fake-tit, void-of-personality Barbie doll that I had been expecting, she was a whisky-drinking, curly-haired firecracker. She poured us a drink, and we sat in the kitchen exchanging pleasantries before taking a tour of the house. The living room furniture looked like it belonged in a modern art museum—fuzzy textures, wild patterns and colors, and strange shapes contrasted wildly with the cold concrete that comprised the floors, ceiling, and walls. The dining room sat between two floor-to-ceiling sliding glass panes that allowed for a breeze to fully pass through the room while the folding glass walls on the entire east side of the structure let it meld into nature. The concrete house was the definition of modern.

Eventually, Collin offered to give us a tour of his property, which included a pond, a pool, a pool house, and a vast expanse of forested land. During the tour, I quickly discovered that Collin, my date, and Ally were all of the meditation sort, which means that they harbor the same sort of enthusiasm as cross fitters and vegans. Mainly, they wouldn't shut up about meditation.

There was one thing that should have tipped me off that this was not going to be a normal night. While Collin showed us around the property, taking us deep into the forest via a dirt path that crossed a rushing stream full of fish, I noticed that the nature noises sounded a little too serene. I scanned the forest, only to discover the presence of several cleverly disguised speakers hidden in trees and rock crevices. And yes, it was exactly what you are thinking. I don't know if the songbirds weren't doing their job, if the trickle of the stream was insufficient, or if the insects weren't buzzing loudly enough, but Collin was actually piping nature sounds into fucking nature. The forest, apparently, was not forest-y enough. I didn't point this out, and no one else seemed to notice.

After emerging from the woods, we retired to the kitchen to prepare dinner. It was late in the evening by this time: the sky was black and the stars were out. That's one thing that rural areas have on cities—the quietness and star-dotted black beauty of the night sky. We had dinner in the living room, with both glass walls wide open and a candle chandelier providing our only source of light. The nature sounds persisted, mostly due to the surrounding speakers, but aided by random insects that flew past. When dessert was finished and our wine glasses were topped up, Collin suggested that we head to the pool house. I grabbed the bottle of wine and we walked through the night-darkened grass towards the iron railing that fenced in the pool and the accompanying pool house. Just as Collin reached the gate, he pulled out his phone, unlocked it, hit a few buttons, and suddenly the entire pool area erupted into a symphony of the most offensive rap music I had ever heard in my entire life. The contrast between what had been playing seconds before and the music that now blasted through the speakers was confusing. The mood had gone from serene to club scene in 2.5 seconds.

We passed through the gates and into the dimly-lit pool grounds. I headed for the hot tub that was situated near the far end of the pool and offered up a view of the now black forest. I pulled the hem of my dress a little further up my knees, slipped my feet out of my shoes, and stepped into the hot tub, taking a seat on the outer side and setting my wine glass down beside me. No sooner had I taken a sip and glanced behind me than I saw Collin and Ally. Both of them had disrobed and were standing there, buck-ass naked.

I paused for a moment to process this and watched Collin and Ally jump into the pool. *Whatever,* I thought. It was Collin's property. If he wanted to be naked on a Saturday night and go skinny dipping in his pool, more power to him. I turned my attention to my date and I watched as he, too, disrobed to the point of nakedness.

This was strange. But then again, I already knew that they were meditation enthusiasts. Maybe being naked was a part of their deal?

My naked date slid into the hot tub beside me while I sat on the side and dangled my legs in the water. I chanced a glance back at the pool and saw Collin and Ally, darkly-lit, in a full-on make-out session. At that point, my date asked me if I wanted to take my clothes off. Being naïve (or stupid, whatever you want to call it) I did not comprehend the implications of this request. I just thought it was strange, and I didn't want to get roped into their naked meditation cult. I had tried meditation before and it was not for me, and I didn't think that being naked would improve my opinion of it.

"No," I smiled. "I'm good."

Ten minutes later, a naked Collin and Ally both joined us in the hot tub. Ally sat on the edge like me while Collin stood in the water, in between her legs. We chatted amicably while Collin and Ally proceeded to get busy with each other in front of my date and me. Again, I thought it was strange, but if exhibitionism was their thing, who was I to stop them?

My date came over and started feeling up my legs, but, while I was comfortable having two people get down and dirty beside me, I was not comfortable being groped beside them. I brushed off my date, drank some more wine, and we eventually settled into an easy conversation. Then, Collin turned to my date and me and asked if we wanted to retire to the pool house for a bit. I was thoroughly enjoying the contrast between the crisp summer air and the warm water on my legs, as well as the ink-black sky and bright twinkling stars. I declined, but my date was up for it. And so, the three of them retired to the pool house for twenty-ish minutes while I sat on the edge of the hot tub, drank wine, listened to shitty rap music, and gazed at the night sky.

Perhaps others would have caught on more quickly than I did, but I had no inkling that anything untoward was occurring in the pool house. I still just thought that they were weird meditation people who enjoyed being naked. When the threesome reappeared, I had no idea what they had been doing. *Mixing more drinks,* I thought innocently. They climbed into the hot tub again and we eventually headed back to the house. By this point, it was around 1 a.m. and my date and I had decided that we were spending the night. We retired to a room upstairs, and I fell asleep on my usual side of the bed, with my date lying beside me.

I woke up the next morning, with the sun beaming into the bedroom and my head hazy from the night before. I scrunched my eyes up in an attempt to avoid the light and glanced over, only to discover that my date was gone and that his side of the bed did not appear to have been slept in. I was confused by this, so I got up to search for him. I found him asleep in a different room and, when he woke up, I questioned why he had abandoned me.

"You were stretched out and took up the whole bed," he said. "There was barely any room for me."

Immediately I knew that my date was full of shit. I know from previous boyfriends and from my sleeping habits that I stick to the edge of whichever side of the bed I am on. I barely move in the middle of the night, I am exceedingly quiet, and I always sleep curled up on my side. Babycakes told me that most of the time he forgot that I was actually sleeping next to him—but this may also have had something to do with how much liquor he drank before bed.

My date and I went out and grabbed coffee and breakfast and brought it back for Collin and Ally before we headed back into the city. The entire time, I was trying to figure out why my date had slept in a different bed and why he had lied about the reason behind it.

I met up for a late brunch with my friends the following day and relayed to them the strange story of the previous evening. I was met with looks of incredulity, and one of my friends finally blurted out what was apparently exceedingly obvious to everyone at the table except for me: my date, Collin, and Ally had been angling for a foursome, but I was too naïve to know it.

Of course, once my friend vocalized it, it all clicked. I

felt like Cher from *Clueless*. And I suddenly realized *why* my date had not slept next to me and *why* he had lied about it. And I realized what the three of them had been doing in the pool house. They hadn't been getting drinks. They had been getting off.

But I wasn't upset, I wasn't indignant, I wasn't put-off. I was intrigued. Who tries to spring a surprise foursome on someone on a second date? Apparently, the men I date.

Having read this far into the book, it's perhaps unsurprising to learn that I went out with him again. When he picked me up, I asked him why he thought it was appropriate to spring a surprise foursome on me, and why he did not think it pertinent to ask me in advance if I was into it. This would have ensured that at least I knew what was going on and, who knows, maybe I would have actually participated. He was evasive and suggested, again, that we drive up to Collin's estate that evening.

I declined.

BABYCAKES 6

Babycakes was in the city for business one cold Wednesday during winter. He had started off his day with a breakfast Caesar, which marked it as a particularly good morning. I was working until five, and Babycakes had a packed schedule. It culminated in meeting with a handful of commercial bankers at 4 p.m.

Now, if you don't happen to know much about bankers or finance as a whole, there really is only one thing that you need to know, and that one thing is what fuels the industry—namely, liquor. Don't get me wrong, egos, women, and money are a part of it, too, but alcohol is at the very bottom of Maslow's Hierarchy of Bankers' Needs. Right there beside food, cocaine, and water.

When Babycakes is amongst bankers, he is in good company. Trying to pick a sober one out of the bunch is like trying to pick out your favorite snowflake in the sky— it's impossible. "Meetings" typically consist of going to a bar, throwing back drinks, and bullshitting. And because of this, I was concerned about what kind of shape Babycakes would be in afterwards.

I texted him around 4:30 p.m., eager to figure out a plan for the night.

What's the plan, Babycakes? I messaged him before realizing I had forgotten to add in something important.

He read my text immediately and began typing.

And please don't get drunk with the bankers, I added and pressed send, to which a simultaneous response from Babycakes popped up on my screen: *Getting drunk with the bankers.*

I let out a sigh.

Not unexpected, but still.

Babycakes showed up two hours later, looking distinctly toasty.

"How many drinks did you have?" I questioned him.

"Two!" he said jovially.

I eyed him suspiciously but said nothing. I would bet my first-born child that Babycakes had consumed more than two drinks, but I had no evidence to back up my case. It turned out that I didn't need to, as Babycakes told on himself at the next bar that we went to. He liked one particular bartender and offered up that he had been overserved earlier and had three glasses of wine. But "three glasses" meant more like five. The bar that he had been at was notorious for topping up each nine-ounce glass with "just a splash" to satiate the alcohol appetite of the Bay Streeters.

My mental tally put Babycakes at *at least* one full bottle of wine to himself—approximately five drinks in total. But that did not stop him from promptly ordering up a beer. He stayed away from hard liquor that night, and by the time we went to bed, Babycakes had consumed one bottle of wine and six beers over the course of the evening. Eleven drinks in total.

When he woke up the next morning, he was perky and

feeling fresh as a daisy.

"First time in in a long time I haven't woken up with a hangover," he remarked with a grin.

Eleven drinks. On a Wednesday. And no next-day hangover. I would have been dry-heaving in the hospital while hooked up to an I.V. But not Babycakes. He was proud that he had shown restraint and had not gone on to drink hard liquor. His reward to himself for his good behavior? A breakfast Caesar—to start the morning off right.

THAT TIME I UNWITTINGLY BECAME A
FINANCIAL DOMINATRIX

I don't know how often this happens to other people, but in a typical year, I usually field texts from at least five unknown numbers. And I'm not talking "We met at the bar last night when I was blacked out" unknown numbers or people trying to run a scam. I'm talking truly bizarre shit.

One winter, I received one such text. *Goddess*, it read, *I long for you to control my spending.*

I glanced at the message, furrowed my brow, and said, "What the fuck." At the same time, I was intrigued and clicked on the message. I didn't have any previous texts from this phone number, the area code of which indicated that the texter lived in my city. I did not have any previous phone calls from this phone number either. The only thing that made sense to me was that someone had accidentally texted the wrong number, or someone had texted the right number—someone had just given them the wrong one. And if ever there were a more-right number for someone to accidentally text about becoming a financial dominatrix, mine was it.

Control your spending? I texted back.

Yes, Goddess. I want to serve you. I want you to tell me how to spend it. I want to buy you things.

I was past the WTF stage at this point and had moved into full fits of giggles. Some random man wanted me to control his spending and buy me shit. Now, were I a Machiavellian type, I could have bankrupted him. Fortunately for him and his bank account, I am not. I did have a bit of fun, though. We texted back and forth for a few weeks while he begged me to financially dominate him.

Goddess, he wrote one afternoon, *I want to buy you shoes. Pick out a pair from this website.* What followed was a link to a site selling some fun high heels. They weren't Louboutins or anything, but they were cute and reasonably priced. Given that he was offering it to me and that I knew that he was getting something out of it—sexual gratification—I acquiesced and picked out a couple of pairs.

I texted him back links to two pairs of shoes that I quite liked. *Size 8. Send them to this store,* I texted. *Of course,* I didn't have them sent to my home. I didn't even know this person. Although given his insistence that he buy me shoes, there was a fair chance that *he* actually knew who *I* was. All I knew was that things were going to get awkward when I showed up at the store to pick up the pumps and I could not provide photo I.D. proof that my name was "Goddess."

This weird financial-dominatrix-texting thing went on for a few more weeks until I stopped responding. Sure, the guy was getting his rocks off and I was getting seriously entertained, but the novelty had worn off. At the same time, I was concerned that he was going to get himself into financial trouble if he tried the same shit with someone who had less scruples. So, before I stopped responding, I got him to agree to never spend more than $500 per month on a "Goddess." There are some truly terrible people out there and he was bound to find someone who would end up putting him into bankruptcy.

Sadly, some things remain a mystery. I never did find out who my financial submissive was or how he got my number. Or whether he found a woman with less integrity than I and ended up filing for Chapter 7.

BABYCAKES 7

One evening, I decided that it would be fun for us to visit a sex club. But I wasn't looking at it from a sexual point of view, it was purely for entertainment purposes. During dinner, I told Babycakes where I wanted to take him that night. We were both dressed up—him in his requisite suit, me in my high heels and cocktail dress. He didn't seem thrilled with the idea, but he also didn't seem entirely opposed to it. I told him that, if nothing else, the club had a bar.

He agreed to go.

When we flagged down a cab and rattled off our destination, the driver immediately started laughing his ass off. He tried to keep his composure as we drove through the streets, but couldn't contain the guffaws. Babycakes, who up until this point I thought was immune to embarrassment, actually seemed a little mortified.

This was interesting.

After paying the bemused driver, we opened the door to the club, which is situated in an old, four-story house, and walked down the stairs. The place didn't appear to be packed. It didn't appear to have *any* patrons, in fact. I should mention that it was Tuesday, which, apparently, was cheap night. It was also the first Tuesday of the month which, we discovered, meant that it was also "foot fetish night." I was not aware of this when I decided that we should go to the sex club that evening and, coincidentally, I was wearing a very sexy, very high pair of Louboutins.

They made us provide an email address to register that night and Babycakes paid the fee. He did not, however, allow them to use his email address. He made me give them mine instead. They gave us each one towel and the key to a locker and told us to have fun.

We stood there awkwardly in the main room, just off the entrance. Both of us were dressed to the nines, clutching white towels, and looking around awkwardly as hardcore porn played on multiple TVs around the room.

There was one other person standing there beside us, a woman who was wearing not a lot of clothing—to be expected at a sex club. She could see that we were clearly out of our element and unsure of what to do, so she came over, introduced herself, and offered to give us a tour.

I believe her name was Cathy. And even if it wasn't, that's what I'm going to call her. Cathy started out by explaining that it was permissible for us to have sex absolutely everywhere—everywhere except for the hot tub.

Cathy then proceeded to show us around the place, meticulously taking us room to room, explaining what each of them was for. After walking up to the second floor and showing us where the lockers were, we followed her around, still fully clothed and clutching our towels like they were some sort of sex-club patron-repellant talismans.

While the first floor had been virtually devoid of people, cheap night apparently brings out the crowds on floor two. It also brings out the foot fetish enthusiasts, which was evidenced by the number of times I was complimented on my shoes.

But Cathy was all business.

"This is the stripper room," she said, gesturing towards a room that contained a bar, a long bench across one wall, and a stripper pole. "This is the gang-bang room," she said nonchalantly, gesturing into the smaller room that contained red plastic beds with gang-bang porno playing on the TVs.

I've experienced a lot in my life, but the thought of there being a designated room for gang-bangs sent me over the edge. Internally, I was dying. Externally, I somehow maintained my composure. Then I looked at Babycakes: he actually looked scared.

I died inside even more.

Cathy finished the rest of the tour, taking us up to the third floor which contained a dungeon, more rooms with red plastic beds that were not exclusively for gang-bangs, a room with a VW Beetle in it that had a mattress in the back, and finally, to the fourth floor, which looked like a bedroom in a crack house and came complete with a Port-a-Potty-style "Occupied/Vacant" switch.

At this point, Babycakes needed a drink. We went down to the locker room, disrobed, wrapped ourselves in towels, and headed for the bar. Babycakes wanted to go and was more interested in his liquor, but I wanted to see more. So, we wandered into the dungeon and, after a quick glance around, I sat down, dragging Babycakes onto the bench beside me.

Strapped to a wooden table on one end of the dark and dreary room was a naked, 300-pound man wearing nothing but a ponytail and sideburns. He was being whipped by an equally round woman wearing black leather, and every time this woman's whip would lash across his body, this man would moan like he was eating the best steak of his life.

I was mesmerized.

Beside the whipping table, on some sort of squishy props, sat a woman in her early twenties and a silver-haired man. Both of them were buck-ass naked and eating—I shit you not—a pizza. An. Entire. Pizza. Delivery box and all. Right beside a naked man being whipped on a table. And beside the pizza-eating man and woman? A trio of furries! Three furries, all buck-ass naked, but clearly furries by their mascot heads. Three foxes, each one a different color.

I don't think Babycakes could process all this. It was too much for him. He looked both scared and confused—his nervous system had taken over and his body had chosen flight.

I, on the other hand, was in my element.

There may be only one thing that I enjoy more than watching people in their natural environments. And that one thing is taking people out of their comfort zones, putting them into uncomfortable zones, and watching it play out.

Babycakes and I left shortly after that, much to my dismay, but I will never forget the look of fear on his face as he sat there in his towel, desperately clutching his beer to his body like some sort of shield. Somehow, I had convinced my staunch Republican paramour to attend a gay bar and now a sex club. One small step for Babycakes, one giant leap for Babycakes' kind. And all it took was the promise of liquor. If only the rest of society was so simple. World wars could be prevented with enough vodka.

DOCTOR DAN

I found Doctor Dan on Tinder. His profile only had one photo: the crest of a highly-regarded, Ivy-league university. He described himself as a prominent and dominant plastic surgeon who was looking for a submissive. Always up for an interesting conversation or experience, I swiped right and we matched.

Messages were exchanged over several days, but there was one problem. Dan refused to send me any photos of himself, citing concerns about being a prominent figure in the city who needed to protect his privacy. I entertained this logic for a while, but it started to make me uneasy. After all, what kind of weirdo won't send someone a photo after several days of talking? Or maybe a better question would be: what kind of woman continues to communicate with a man who won't send her photos after several days of talking?

I am a very busy man, he wrote. *Let's set up a time to talk.* So, we did—for the following Sunday at 1 p.m. I ended up sleeping off a hangover that afternoon and my phone was on silent so I missed his call. It was when I awoke that I realized that Dr. Dan had multiple phone numbers. There was a missed call from one and text messages from another. Neither of those numbers were registered to WhatsApp, which I found strange, but we rescheduled our call for later that week.

I was awake when he called this time, and I was surprised by what I heard on the other end of the line—a high-pitched, nasally voice. Far from the alpha male that he had purported himself to be, Dan sounded like a prepubescent, male-version of Fran Drescher. This was difficult for me to square away. He boasted about being the biggest alpha in the room while his voice gave me visions of Barry Gibb in a dress. It was not a turn-on.

"There are articles written about me," Dan bragged. "They say, 'He is the kind of man who gets what he wants fifteen seconds before he knows he wants it.' "

I shook with silent laughter on the other end of the line but said nothing.

"Have you ever been with a man of my stature?" he demanded.

I rolled my eyes and said I had.

"There was another article written about me," he went on. "It said 'If there was an alpha male conference, Dan would be the keynote speaker.' "

Again, words failed me.

Dan questioned me about being submissive.

"I love to make my partner happy," I told him. "When my partner is happy, I'm happy."

"I need to know if you can pleasure me," he responded, "if I tell you to take me in your mouth."

At this I stuffed a pillow in my face to stifle my laughter.

Dan seemed to be sending a bunch of non-sequiturs my way to see how I would respond. Most of the time I said nothing, which seemed to suit him fine.

By the end of the call, Dan told me that he was going to leave it to me to text him and let him know if I wanted to have another phone call. I could tell at this point that he was hooked, which was strange as I had barely said anything to him during the course of our conversation. It seemed that Doctor Dan, in addition to being a "dominant alpha male," also got turned on by the sound of his own voice. I imagined foreplay with him consisted of one giant Dan monologue while he jerked himself off. Probably while staring at himself in the mirror.

Was Dan even looking for a partner? I pondered. Maybe he just liked having conversations with unwitting women where he boasted about his greatness and allowed them to bask, momentarily, in his glory. The thought that Dan had probably hung up the phone and immediately gotten off on himself flitted through my head.

Two days later, as I had anticipated, Dan could not take my silence and he sent me a text. *So, are we having another call?*

I was amused. Dan had painted himself as a dominant male and had ostensibly left the ball in my court. But when it came down to it, his indifference only lasted two days. This broke any remaining notions I had of his dominant persona. A man who was truly in control, I reasoned, would have waited for me to come to them.

Eventually I told Dan that, given he wouldn't even send me a picture, I didn't think that things were going anywhere and declined a second phone call. He seemed to find this funny.

I am not entirely convinced that I didn't miss out on a date with Patrick Bateman, the murderous villain from *American Psycho*. Which leads me to another thing that I've learned—if you have the slightest inkling that you need to tell close friends and family where you are going and with whom because you have concerns about your safety, you probably shouldn't be going on a date with this person in the first place. Although Lord knows Dan would probably be an easy one to escape from. All you would have to do is hold up any surface with a modicum of reflection and let Narcissus sabotage himself: *"Foiled again!,"* I pictured a dress-wearing Barry Gibb exclaim as he stared at his reflection in a spoon.

BABYCAKES 8

In an effort to save our relationship, which was floundering for the fourteenth time, I suggested that we take a trip. But this is Babycakes we are talking about. I couldn't take him to a relaxing resort, a quaint beach town, or a mountain hideaway—he required places where he could satisfy his addictions. To that end, I settled on Las Vegas to act as our relationship Switzerland. If I was going to claw our twosome out of the dumpster-fire in which it resided, it was going to take a lot of liquor, depravity, and gambling to get there.

I woke up the morning of my flight and discovered that I was having breathing problems. Being a bit neurotic, I decided to take a quick trip to the ER at my local hospital prior to boarding. For some reason I was concerned that I had a collapsed lung, and all of my Googling assured me that the last thing I wanted to do with a collapsed lung was get on an airplane. At the ER, I was X-rayed and discovered that I did not have a collapsed lung—I had a mild case of pericarditis. I was relieved. But I should not have been. I should have taken it as a sign.

Because of my ER side trip, I missed my flight and the only subsequent flight I could take would put me into Sin City at midnight, which meant I probably would not get to the hotel until 1 a.m. This would mean that Babycakes would have ten solid hours in Las Vegas with no one there to rein in his addictions, which would allow him to indulge his inner hedonist while he waited for me to arrive.

That is exactly what occurred.

When I arrived at the Wynn (1 a.m., as expected), I walked in the lobby bar to find Babycakes so liquored up that he could barely speak English. He flopped around on one of the couches like a half-alive fish while he tried to explain to me what had happened. I wasn't quite able to understand the details of his experience, but it all boiled down to three things: Babycakes, alcohol, and blackjack.

I was actually amazed when, after his explanation ended, he called to the bartender and ordered another drink. My amazement was for two reasons: 1. Despite apparently being more alcohol than man and clearly going to be in for a world of pain in six short hours, he was actually going for another drink. 2. The bartender was able to comprehend his drink order. Of course, that may have been because he had been the bar's best customer that evening.

One drink later and Babycakes went full flounder. I helped him into the elevator, and we went upstairs to bed where I said a silent prayer that the next day would be more promising.

In case you were wondering, it wasn't.

Being, as I mentioned earlier, a trip that was meant to rekindle the flame on the Diptyque candle of our love and put out the dumpster-fire reality of our relationship, I had created an itinerary and booked romantic restaurants for breakfast, lunch, and dinner, as well as some fun Las Vegas shows. But, as they say, the best laid plans go awry. Or, in Babycakes' land, the best laid plans go to rye.

As I predicted, Babycakes woke up four hours later with an unholy hangover. His eyes were the color of fruit punch, and his skin had a sickly, white pallor. I won't even get into the smell, but that, fortunately, was something that a quick shower was able to fix. We made it downstairs and were on our way to breakfast when he got side-tracked by a bar that had slot machines at every seat. He had clearly not satiated the betting beast the evening before and saddled up to a seat, threw some money into the machine, and ordered up a Bloody Mary. Breakfast, as it were, was served.

I should have known at this point that sometimes you just have to let something go. Our relationship was a rusted-out '89 Volvo that had a leaky oil tank, a window that wasn't closing, two flat tires, bullet holes, and a door that was falling off. But did I opt for an upgrade? Did I dump the Volvo and go in search of a more reliable vehicle? Something less embarrassing that would bring me safety and comfort? Of course not. Slap some duct-tape on that door, spray some paint over that rust, and ride those rims into the ground.

When I like something, I *really* like something. Even when it's not working for me.

After a liquid breakfast, we ventured out into the hot Las Vegas sun. Too hot, in fact, which led to us scurrying back inside and continuing on with Babycakes' favorite pastimes: drinking and playing blackjack.

We had lunch reservations at Paris Paris—a romantic restaurant with red velvet upholstery and a beautiful view of the strip. Instead, we walked next door and hit up Señor Frog's, where we drank margaritas and got a souvenir photo of me wearing a sombrero and the facial expression you typically see on a hostage, and him holding a long-legged stuffed frog and grinning gleefully from ear to ear.

We drank and gambled all through the shows that I had booked, missing each and every one of them. My frown deepened with each cancelled booking while Babycakes' smile grew brighter and his eyes more glazed over with each passing hour. We may have cancelled Cirque, O, and Absinthe, but there was one reservation that I was absolutely, positively going to keep, and that was dinner at Costa Di Mare.

Costa Di Mare was a gorgeous seafood restaurant at the Wynn, with an outdoor seating area that wrapped around an ankle-deep pond filled with large, shiny metal spheres that popped half-out of the water. The tables were situated far apart under individual fabric canopies and open gazebos, and a lush green wall surrounded the dining area in a semi-circle, lending an exotic feel to the place. In terms of romance, the place was an eleven on a ten scale.

We made it to the upstairs bar and ordered a cocktail before our reservation. Babycakes, solidly liquored up at this point, was unimpressed until we were led downstairs and out onto the patio, at which point even he had to admit he was dazzled.

Our table was located near the middle of the pond, a good thirty-second walk from the doors, and it was a crystal-clear evening—we couldn't have asked for nicer weather. The waiter pulled out my chair as Babycakes began to scan the wine menu. I let my guard down at this point and actually started to feel some stirrings of relaxation and hope. Maybe our three-day relationship saver of a trip would be salvageable after all?

The waiter came back and took our drink orders, returning very quickly with my beer and his vodka, which we clinked together and drank—smiling at each other as we set down our glasses. This was it. We were going to get that old feeling back and right our relationship train that had fallen off the tracks.

But it was at precisely this moment that a higher power intervened and the relationship train, instead of righting itself, went right over a cliff. Jesus, it seems, was quite pissed. *This relationship isn't going to work,* He was telling me. I needed to stop trying. I needed to stop pouring gasoline on the fire and let it burn itself out. How many signs had He sent me? And how many signs had I stubbornly refused to read? Jesus was about to give me a sign that I could not ignore.

I sat there smiling at Babycakes, my fingers resting on my glass, when the sky suddenly blackened, the heavens opened up, and what I can only describe as a monsoon erupted. The winds swept up so hard and fast that glasses blew off of the tables around us. Tablecloths blew in the wind, throwing cutlery off of the tables in every direction like culinary missiles. The rain came down so hard that diners sat there with stunned looks on their faces while their brains tried to process what had just happened. Napkins blew off peoples' laps and into the pond, patrons grabbed their meals and ran like Usain for the doors. In under thirty seconds, I was completely drenched. I actually think I still had that smile on my face, it all happened so quickly. Babycakes and I grabbed our drinks, put menus over our heads in a futile effort to block the rest of the rain, and dodged cutlery, napkins, and broken glass as we legged it for indoors.

Incredibly, I still retained some hope at this point. Okay, our reservation had been a complete disaster, I had mascara running down my face and now resembled that black-haired chick from *The Ring*, but the waiter found us a very nice table right beside the window, which provided us with a clear vantage point of the disaster that was unfolding outside. It might be romantic to be warm and safe inside while eating dinner by candlelight. I watched as napkins blew around outside and tablecloths fluttered violently in the wind. Soggy serviettes floated in the pond and rain battered the piss out of the entire area, slapping the window like a vehicle in a carwash.

Still, I persisted.

Babycakes ordered the fish while I ordered pasta. No sooner did the waiter walk away to put in our orders than Babycakes began nodding off. He was, if you recall, massively hungover from the previous evening, and had, if you recall, only four hours of sleep. Our dinner reservation had been for 9 p.m., so his sleepiness was perhaps understandable if not quite forgivable. By the time his order came (a fish that was placed in front of me, with its face still attached), his head drooped so low in his meal that I was actually concerned he was going to suffocate himself in his fillet.

I finally gave it to Jesus that he might be onto something at this point and acknowledged that maybe this relationship wasn't something worth saving. At any rate, it resulted in a three-month estrangement that merely demonstrated neither of us could keep away from the other.

THREE MEN WALK INTO A BAR

One Saturday evening a girlfriend and I met up for a night out. We didn't have anything crazy planned, just a couple of cocktails at the Shangri-La. It was the middle of winter, and the hotel's lobby lounge wasn't busy. We found ourselves two seats at the bar and ordered up a round of drinks.

While we chatted, I watched out of the corner of my eye as a black-clad man stumbled drunkenly towards us. He grabbed a seat two chairs down and a beer was placed in front of him in short order. It was clear that another drink was the last thing that he needed. His eyes were as red as rubies and, while his proverbial lights were on, no one appeared to be home.

I turned to my friend, eager to catch up: "So, what's going on in your dating life?"

"Well," she said loudly, leaning back in her chair. "I was dating a refugee and a venture capitalist. So, *of course* I went for the one who is rich."

The drunkard two seats down had clearly been eavesdropping; he was mid-drink when my friend made her confession, and he spat out his beer and began laughing his ass off. Loudly. The bartender smirked; I cringed.

I love my girlfriend, but I could not believe that she had just said that. Think it all you want, but dear god, keep that kind of thing to yourself. I didn't want any men to associate me with that type of thinking.

She shot the drunkard an icy glare while he continued to cackle, and I watched as three well-dressed men made their way towards us. They were all wearing wool coats in different shades of dark and one of them, a man in a gray peacoat, appeared to be so drunk that his friends were having to hold him up. They led him, swaying to-and-fro, to the bar and helped him into a chair. It was barely 8 p.m. and yet one-half of the men seated around us were hammered.

The trio engaged us in conversation almost immediately—my friend and I were the only women at the bar, and it didn't take long before one of them walked over. Appearance-wise, he was short, squat, and slightly senior. He wore a smart navy sweater, square, black-rimmed glasses, and had a close-cropped brush of white hair.

"Your friend is hammered, holy shit," I commented on the friend that the senior had helped into a seat.

"No," the senior said. "He's not drunk. He's blind. He left his guide dog at home."

His friend was blind and, given the hard liquor in front of him, he would soon be drunk. A blind drunk. Is that where the term that encompasses next-level inebriation had been coined, I pondered? I found this funny, but I didn't say anything.

The senior's two buddies eventually made their way over to us, with the blind one being steered by his guide-dog understudy—the guide friend. They introduced themselves—Mitchell was the well-dressed senior. He was an entrepreneur and in finance. The other two were named Ezra and Jared, and they were both lawyers. All three of them were out, apparently, for a random night on the town.

Ezra and Jared were polite, respectful, and polished. This made their third wheel all the more curious. Mitchell, the senior, was a bit of a letch. He was shameless in his sexual advances and unrefined in his approach.

While my friend chatted with Ezra and Jared, Mitchell leaned in close to me and did something with his eyes that I suppose he thought was sexy.

"Do you want to do some cocaine?" he looked at me enticingly. I grimaced as I watched sweat roll down the side of his head. I did not want to do some cocaine and turned back to the conversation with his friends. It turned out that the two of them were federal prosecutors who specialized in terrorism and gangs. They had prosecuted some of the highest-profile terrorism cases in the country. *Was there a hotline I could call to report Mitchell,* I wondered? While I didn't think that his behavior quite met the threshold for prosecution, I felt terrorized by his advances.

Undeterred by my snub, Mitchell took a quick trip to powder his nose and then came back for round two. With drugs being stricken from the list, he went the financial route in his second attempt to woo me. He lived in an exclusive and nauseatingly-expensive area of the city—a place where mansions were worth tens of millions of dollars and housed the wealthiest people in all of Canada. Given my friend's admission earlier that evening, I thought that Mitchell probably would have had more success had he told her. But personally? I didn't give two fucks about his postal code.

I could see the frustration building on Mitchell's face as he failed to make inroads with me. But his features quickly softened as he geared up to try another tactic.

"I just want you to know," he said seductively, looking deep into my eyes, "I've had a vasectomy."

As far as pick-up lines went, this was the worst that I had ever heard. I would have rather had Sloth from *The Goonies* ask, "Do you fancy a fuck?" than have a rotund senior insinuate that his inability to procreate should serve as sexual enticement.

Mitchell looked like he expected me to throw myself on top of him. What I *wanted* to do was throw up on him. He was now 0 and 3 but wouldn't let a little thing like dignity stop him from going in for Round Four. He did that weird thing again with his eyes—*maybe it was a tic?*

"I hired a prostitute tonight," he whispered in my ear. "I wouldn't have hired her if I knew that I was going to meet you. I'm going to give her to Jared."

My eyebrows shot to the ceiling. He had purchased a prostitute for the night, but he was going to pawn her off on his friend. Did this count as sloppy seconds? I wasn't sure and excused myself to the washroom to give it more thought.

On my way back, still no nearer to answering the "sloppy seconds" question, I saw a scantily-clad woman cozied up to Jared. It appeared that the prostitute had arrived, and she seemed to be singing in Jared's ear. It looked like he was getting a two-for-one deal, courtesy of his friend—a treat for the aural and oral senses.

This was getting weird.

Mitchell had tried to entice me with his postal code and vasectomy, then pawned off his hooker on a friend. He had openly asked me if I wanted to do cocaine in front of two federal prosecutors and literally purchased a prostitute for one of them. How did Mitchell fit into this friend group, I wondered? He was the polar opposite of the others. What made them mates? When it came to Jared, if he had been hard of hearing, I could understand the friendship. But no, he was only hard of seeing. And I imagined that his heightened sense of hearing meant that the humiliation of his friend's pick-up lines must have been magnified. I wouldn't have been able to look Mitchell in the eye if he were my friend, but then again, neither could Jared.

Regardless, weird is my specialty, and this was the kind of night I could get behind.

After a few drinks, we settled our tab and took a taxi to a popular Mexican bar: me, my friend, Ezra, Mitchell, Jared, and the hooker. My friend and I navigated our way up three flights of stairs while the men took up the rear. When we made it into the bar, I was surprised by what I saw. Latinos are not typically known for their height, but as a taller-than-average woman who was wearing seriously high heels, I could see clear across the packed room. I felt like a giraffe at a meeting of coked-out gophers—which did have one advantage, namely, being able to figure out the best place to get a drink.

We waded into the crowd, and I glanced back to make sure that the entourage was following. They were all there, with Jared being helped along by the seeing-eye prostitute.

"He usually brings his dog," Mitchell confided in me.

The thought of a golden lab wearing his "Working Dog" vest, carting his owner around a bar of drunkards, was too much for me to take.

What would happen if Jared wanted to have a one-night stand? Did his dog also guide him to attractive women? I imagined Jared feeling his way through the crowd and making his way towards a hatchet-faced female. His dog, seeing what his owner could not, would give a firm tug in the opposite direction, leading his owner away from danger. Although, when I really thought about it, I supposed it didn't much matter. In not being able to see, there was no fear of Jared waking up the next morning and wanting to chew his arm off at the sight of his one-night stand. That is one thing the blind have over the sighted— the inability to experience shame based on the sight of what they've picked up at the bar the night before. Her nose could be the fleshy embodiment of an eggplant, and Jared would be none the wiser.

The night progressed in a whirl of drinks and dancing and, at the end of the evening, I gave Ezra my number. Mitchell overheard this and took the opportunity to also save it in his phone. I was into Ezra and hoped to hear from him. He was not, however, into me. I was not into Mitchell and had hoped *not* to hear from him. But I did. One month later, in March 2020, at an ungodly-early hour, I received a text: *What do you say we do a socially-distanced meet up in a parking lot and mutually rub one out,* it read.

Charming.

He was just as appealing via text as he was in person. The pandemic was newly upon us, and Mitchell might just be the last man on Earth I ever had a chance to sleep with.

I never replied.

BABYCAKES 9

I was indulging in cocktails and conversation with some of my girlfriends one evening at my favorite hotel lounge. Drink in hand, I was chatting with a handsome man who was leaning on the bar and regaling me with stories from abroad. Now, because this hotel has played such a prominent role in my life and I've spent so much time there, it is perhaps unsurprising that most of the staff knew me, if not by name, certainly by sight. And, consequently, they knew my boyfriend, Babycakes. I was laughing at something the handsome man was telling me when the bartender leaned over the bar and informed me that Babycakes was outside, drunkenly demanding to be let in. I later found out that Babycakes was denied entry when the bouncer asked him how many drinks he had had that evening and he belligerently answered, "Fifteen."

After being denied entry, Babycakes then went downstairs and drunkenly complained to the front-desk staff, using the tired old, "Do you know who I am?" trope.

"Yes, Mr. Babycakes," the front-desk clerk had said calmly. "I understand, you are a very important guest." She then dialed the upstairs bar and asked that Babycakes be let in. He was denied for the second time that evening, this time through the front-desk-clerk intermediary.

For the average person, it would be embarrassing, but Babycakes was unashamed. He went downstairs the next morning and apologized to the front-desk staff for his behavior and, that evening, he went upstairs and apologized to the bouncer. That's Babycakes—demanding and belligerent one minute and apologizing unreservedly the next. He is nothing if not diplomatic. Especially if the situation could possibly come between him and his liquor.

UN-ORTHODOX

I met him in the upstairs bar at a hotel. An entertainment group had taken over management of the bar, which subsequently saw it turned into a party Thursday through Saturday night, complete with women wearing blonde wigs and skimpy black dresses. It was the hottest ticket around for a few months, with people waiting tens of minutes in the lobby to enter into one of the four elevators that would bring them to the 31st floor. It was there, with one of my girlfriends who seemingly knew everyone in the city, that I was introduced to him.

He was my height, with a Jason Statham-esque face and air about him, clad in a sleek, black suit and sporting an Aussie accent. I should preface this by saying that, while he is the one with whom I went on several dates, it is his friend who provided the inspiration for this chapter's title.

Mason, the Jason Statham clone, was an entrepreneur who worked downtown. I didn't catch the specifics, but if my girlfriend gave him the green light, I was pedal-to-the-metal go. A complete gentleman, Mason grabbed my hand and ordered me a drink, regaling me with his irresistible accent and chivalrous charm. Despite this, there was one thing that I found strange—every few minutes Mason would look deep into my eyes with a smouldering smile and say: "What's your name, love? Tell me, what's your name?"

I couldn't quite tell where this question was coming from, and I wasn't entirely sure if it was a question or a statement. Did he have transient amnesia that only pertained to my name? (He had been following our entire conversation quite clearly throughout the evening.) Did he genuinely not remember my name? Was this some form of flirting I wasn't familiar with? The "What's your name, love? Tell me, what's your name?" thing continued on throughout our short time together.

For most of the night, Mason's best friend stood beside him—a lean, six-foot-tall man with Hasidic Jew side-curls, a black hat, and a black suit—drinking hard liquor. John, the Orthodox Jew who appeared to be having an identity crisis, threatened to kill me if I hurt his friend. And not just general "I will kill you if you hurt him" type of talk, but alarming specifics: "I will stab you with a butcher knife and then run you over with my car" type of specifics. My eyebrows could not have risen any higher. John's appearance, alcohol notwithstanding, indicated that he was a simple man of God. His speech and drink, on the other hand, indicated that he was an educated degenerate with a penchant for irony.

As the evening wore on, Mason and I flirted at the bar and engaged in deep conversation. The lights and liquor danced around us until the bartenders began to shut things down. Mason grabbed a taxi and dropped me off at the lobby of my building that evening, sealing the night with a kiss and promising to see me later that week.

We made dinner plans for that Thursday on a quaint but lively street that hosted a strip of popular restaurants. Being a bit particular when it comes to what I eat, I assumed mine would be a meal that consisted of bread and vegetables. Mason had decided to take me to a Greek restaurant that, while highly rated, had a sparse menu. For some reason, he neglected to tell me that this would be a double date—with John, the un-Orthodox Jew, and his lover, Angelica.

I say "lover" and not "girlfriend", "friend with benefits", or "date" because this was literally how I was introduced to Angelica. When we arrived at the restaurant, John and Angelica were already there, seated on one side of the table.

"This is my lover, Angelica," John said, running his hand across the blonde's shoulder.

I sat down across from her while Mason sat across from John, who was still sporting the side-curls, black suit, and black hat that ostensibly revealed him as a man of God. And if John's appearance represented all that is holy, Angelica was his equal and opposite in sin. Long, fake talons, lips injected to the point of bursting, brassy-blonde hair extensions, fake lashes, fake tits, smoky eye-shadow, and a skimpy dress.

Immediately after I took my seat, Angelica leaned across the table conspiratorially to ask me if I wanted to know why her cat's name was John. Bit of an odd conversation opening to be sure, but maybe she was going somewhere interesting with this?

"Sure," I smiled in a friendly manner.

Angelica smiled back—it seemed genuine—and said: "So, John had me bent over the counter and was doing me from behind in the kitchen one day and my cat was on the floor next to us, playing with a blanket." She paused to gauge my reaction before moving on. "And then my cat put his paw around the blanket like he was choking it and I said, 'Hey! That's John's move!', so I re-named my cat John."

It dawned on me at this moment that I was sitting at a table with an Aussie, a Hasidic Jew, and a pervert. It felt like the opening to a bad joke and I wasn't sure if I was going to be the punchline. What does one even say to Angelica's story? *So—Cat John and Orthodox-Jew John are both into BDSM? Interesting.*

The dinner got progressively more strange after that. When the meal came, John proceeded to build the Iron Dome out of cutlery on top of the plate of mashed potatoes while Angelica regaled me with stories of her boyfriend who lived in a different city, paid for all of her things, including her condo—and who didn't know that she was banging John—as well as her stint on a short-lived, reality television show. This was all punctuated by Mason periodically staring deep into my eyes and asking, "What's your name, love? Tell me, what's your name?"

As far as first dates go, I wasn't sure if there was nowhere to go but up or down. In any case, Mason and I went out a couple more times and I thought that we had mutually decided to part ways; our texts dropped off dramatically and I found out he buggered off to his home country. Upon his return one month later, he messaged me, saying that he wanted to see me. We did not see each other again, but I did see John out at the bar once after that—he gave me the evil eye but did not, thankfully, try to stab me with a butcher knife and run me over with his car. This indicated to me, at least, that I hadn't hurt his friend.

The baggage I've brought with me from that liaison has

manifested in me being forced to fight off fits of giggles anytime someone with a particular accent asks me, "What's your name?" and in eyeing apparent religious devotees with suspicion.

BABYCAKES 10

One of Babycakes' clients also became one of his very good friends. I'm going to call him Thomas. He was an incredibly wealthy individual who shared the same love of hedonistic indulgences as Babycakes, and he had more than enough money to back it up. Women, alcohol, women, alcohol. Parties. More women. More alcohol.

The two of them were peas in a pod.

I confess that I was actually quite fond of this friend of his—Thomas was equal parts kind and jovial as he was curmudgeonly and cold. The first time I met him, he asked me if I wanted some milk. I thought that he was teasing me about my age in comparison to Babycakes', but it turns out that "milk" is what he had christened his favorite cocktail—vodka.

Thomas had been one of Babycakes' clients for nearly twenty years and they had been friends for nearly that length of time. Being very elderly, Thomas began to slow down over the years and, inevitably, nature took its course and he passed away.

Babycakes was understandably upset. I felt very sorry for him. Death is difficult. Death is even more difficult when it's a close friend that you've had for twenty years and you're edging closer to the reaper yourself. I consoled him like a good girlfriend would.

Now, recall that Babycakes lived in a different city than me but came to mine on a regular basis for work. Thomas had lived in my city and his funeral was on a Friday. Babycakes, distraught, told me he wouldn't be able to attend. He had an urgent client matter he had to take care of in Florida. The urgent matter? A client was insisting that Babycakes play as his partner in a golf tournament. I was incensed. I understand that wealthy clients can be needy, demanding, and inflexible, but refusing to let your wealth manager attend the funeral of a close friend because you need him as a golf partner?

It was actually believable.

That Friday morning, I texted Babycakes. My heart hurt for him.

On the course, he texted me back. *Wish I was at Thomas' funeral. It's going on right now.*

I felt ill.

Your client is a dick, I responded. *I'm sorry, Babycakes. I feel so awful for you. I can't believe that he wouldn't let you attend the funeral.*

Fast forward six months: Babycakes and I were sitting across from one another at a popular restaurant. Our drinks were in front of us, we had ordered dinner, and we were enjoying each other's company. We were sipping companionably and were getting along. The mood was calm and it was early in the evening so Babycakes wasn't too tipsy. We were discussing random topics when suddenly Babycakes uttered a sentence that would place a black cloud over the rest of the night: "When I was at

Thomas' funeral, we went to that restaurant after."

Wait. What?

When he was at Thomas' funeral? The funeral he was unable to attend? The funeral that he was so distraught over? The funeral that I teared up over because Babycakes wasn't able to say goodbye to his close friend because of a dickhead Floridian client?

My glass hovered mid-air in my hand as I stared at him and processed this revelation—not only had Babycakes not been stuck on a golf course, playing in a tournament for a nasty, ice-hearted client, he had *actually* been in my city, attending the funeral and texting me while he was at the funeral, *pretending* to be playing golf in Florida and *pretending* to be upset that he couldn't attend the funeral.

I was so stunned that I couldn't form a sentence. I just kept staring at him, my glass still hovering in mid-air.

Babycakes tried to deny it, said that I had my days mixed up. Then he claimed that "They held a second funeral." (For all he's intelligent and a master study in the art of lying, sometimes he's really terrible at it.)

I heaved a long sigh, pulled out my phone, and searched our WhatsApp chat for Thomas' name and showed him the text messages he had sent, stating that he was on the golf course in Florida the day of his friend's funeral.

He at least had the decency to look ashamed, which was something that I was unaccustomed to seeing. I could barely believe the gall. The bar was set so low that it had been placed underground by a backhoe and in an astounding act of determination he had clawed his way underground to burrow beneath it.

The rest of our dinner was eaten in silence, but I wasn't angry with him or upset. I was dumbfounded and I genuinely wanted to understand what was wrong with him.

I assumed he just hadn't wanted to bring me to the funeral. I believed it was because he either didn't want people there to see him with me or perhaps he brought someone else (his [ex?]-wife) instead. And instead of telling me that he didn't want me to come, he concocted an elaborate lie to keep me from asking questions.

When I asked him what was wrong with him, Babycakes just said that he's a dick.

I tended to agree.

I SEE DEAD PEOPLE

I met Jimmy at a restaurant when a friend and I were out for dinner one evening. He was a tech worker in his mid-fifties and had pretty blue eyes and an easy smile. He and his friend, Rick, were sitting at the bar, telling entertaining stories to those seated beside them. Rick's stories were hysterical. He embarked upon a fifteen-minute-long monologue about how he had been fired from different jobs while going into detail about each termination, which was always owing to something sexual.

"I worked in the meat department at Publix and then I got fired." He paused while everyone eagerly waited for the punchline. "I got fired for beating my meat!"

The stories continued with jobs that included being a bait master, an arborist, and a mechanic. By mid-to-late evening, helped along by the liquor, his stories had everyone in stitches. At some point, we all decided that we should go for drinks one night. Numbers were exchanged and we promised each other that we would make plans one night soon.

Fast forward three weeks and Jimmy texted me to go

for drinks that same day at a hotel pub near my place. I was not aware that this was a date and only realized that Jimmy considered it to be one when I showed up and he said that he would schedule something ahead of time for our next date instead of asking me at the last minute.

I was not interested in Jimmy as anything more than a friend but I also didn't want to be rude so I said nothing. After a couple of cocktails and general "getting to know you" conversation, we decided to go for dinner. We went to an upscale steakhouse and sat at the bar, which is when things took a turn for the weird. Jimmy was a nice enough man, to be sure, and the conversation was easy, but after he opened up, I felt like I needed a young priest and an old priest . . . and a therapist.

Jimmy turned to me after we clinked our glasses together and took a drink.

"I can see dead people," he said seriously.

I stared at him and waited for the punchline.

It didn't come.

Dead relatives were all around him, Jimmy claimed. He also had premonitions.

"Oh?" I took a sip of my drink and said nothing else.

Jimmy went on.

"Yes," he continued. "I saw my mom being murdered in my dream and when I woke up, my dead relatives were all around me telling me that my mom was in danger."

I kept my face neutral at this point but I was wondering if Jimmy was maybe off of his meds.

"Then I found out that my mother was murdered," he said matter-of-factly. "In real life."

It turns out that Jimmy might actually have some sort of psychic powers. It's a terribly tragic story—Jimmy's mom was murdered by a troubled teenager that she had taken into her home. In trying to be a good person and provide the teen with a stable home, love, and care, she had become his murder victim. It is beyond horrific.

We sat in silence for a few minutes after this. I didn't quite know what to say. Jimmy had told me something that I would not expect someone to reveal on a fourth date let alone on a first. And besides, this wasn't even a date.

The bartender topped up our drinks and our conversation carried on.

"Have you ever been married?" Jimmy asked me, to which I shook my head "no." "I have one ex-wife," he said before launching into what went wrong with his marriage. Which was, chiefly, that his ex-wife had cheated on him. With three different men. All of whom were named Brian.

I fought the urge to chime in that maybe things could have lasted had he only opted for a name change. Instead, I crinkled my eyes and tried to arrange my face into some semblance of sympathy.

"Last year I found out that I have prostate cancer," Jimmy went on, adding that he had been on chemo and it was currently in remission.

I tried to offer up some condolences on everything shitty that had happened in his life, but Jimmy brushed it off and continued.

"I found out two years ago that I have a 20-year-old daughter," he said, revealing that he was now trying to get to know her. "She had had a baby four months ago and now I'm a first-time grandfather."

I sat there mostly in silence and let Jimmy talk. And talk. And talk. The poor man had had a rough few years and it seemed like he needed someone to talk to. I only began to get uncomfortable when Jimmy grabbed my hand. I typically eschew affection until I have really gotten to know someone and we have established that there is something between us. Hand-holding on first dates when I wasn't even aware that I had agreed to go on a first date to begin with was a no-go. Although I did kind of get it—Jimmy had shared a lot about himself with me and it had forged some kind of connection between us. I think it's known as "trauma bonding." Regardless, I am not into holding hands with strangers, so I tried to keep my hand on the bar at all times.

"Why aren't you married?" Jimmy asked—the question that every single woman in her thirties just loves to hear. I could be his next wife, he speculated, seemingly out of nowhere. I wasn't sure if this was information that his dead relatives were giving him, if Jimmy had had a fever dream the night before, or if the mere act of using me like a therapist had forged some kind of matrimonial bond in his mind, but I disagreed. I would have to come and see him at his ranch, he said. After all, we were going to be spending a lot of time together now.

I went home afterwards and told my family about my date. I felt really awful because he had shared so many personal things with me, but I just wasn't into him and I didn't know how to let him down gently.

"Surely you can just turn him down," said my brother-in-law practically. "Let's be real—it sounds like it wouldn't be the worst thing that's happened to him."

Touché.

BABYCAKES 11

There is something really appealing to me about contrasts and opposites. Good with bad, black with white, beauty with ugly, classy with trashy. This story focuses on the latter.

One thing that Babycakes and I started doing in the second year of our relationship was throwing an annual Christmas party. Of course, due to our tendency to break up and make up so often, it went from annual to biennial, to triennial. Regardless, the first year we threw a Christmas party we decided to host it at our favorite piano bar.

The atmosphere was seventies style: dark wood, red carpeting, and other rich, warm tones. Guests were welcomed upstairs with an open bar, appetizers, piano music, and a vintage glamour atmosphere. The wait staff dressed in black suits, and Caesar salads and steaks were prepared table-side. One individual Babycakes invited was a man whose business he was considering investing in. We'll call him Chris.

I mentioned earlier that contrasts appeal to me. So, how, exactly, do you contrast an upscale, suit-clad wait staff, fine dining, piano-bar establishment? You ensure that part two of your Christmas party entails carting off everyone in attendance to the trashiest strip club in the city. White glove service meets glove-up service.

We were spreading the Christmas cheer. Babycakes bought lap dances for some of the guests and we all sat back having drinks while watching scantily clad women undulate on stage.

Babycakes was in fine form that evening, and we were all enjoying ourselves until I looked over and saw Babycakes run past the stage with a stripper clinging to his back. And, no, it wasn't a case of him trying to fight her off. He was happily giving the stripper a piggyback ride. Typical Babycakes. He always had to push the envelope. It's not enough that his girlfriend takes him to a strip club for a Christmas party—he has to take it one step further by letting a stripper ride around on his back. I'm a liberal woman and girlfriend and will let my partner get away with a lot, but in this instance, Babycakes had taken it one step too far.

Later that evening, I was talking with Chris and he invited me to go to his house for dinner later that week. I thanked him for the invitation and said that Babycakes wouldn't be in the city then but that we would love to do so when he returned.

Chris replied that Babycakes didn't have to know and that he wasn't invited.

I told Babycakes the next morning that I didn't trust Chris, that I wouldn't trust him in any business negotiations, and I told him about his dinner invitation to me.

Babycakes, in typical fashion, disregarded my advice and invested in Chris' company anyway, believing that the opportunity to make a few million vastly outweighed his potential business partner disrespectfully hitting on his girlfriend. This decision resulted in hundreds of thousands of dollars that would have been better spent had it been lit on fire, and Babycakes getting exactly nothing in return on his investment. He lost $700,000.

He said it was a bad call.

I said it was karma.

BABYCAKES 12

One night, Babycakes and I were out for dinner. I can't quite recall what we were discussing but at the end of the conversation he told me to go to my favourite jeweler and pick out a necklace.

"Just try and keep it under one hundred grand," he said.

Now, I like jewelry. Not just expensive stuff, but I definitely like the expensive stuff, too. So, as instructed, a couple of days later I went to my favorite jeweler and picked out a diamond necklace. It was $60,000. It was delicate, glittered like a drag queen, and looked exquisite around my neck. Instead of being in gold, silver, or platinum settings, each diamond had a hole drilled through it with metal wire wrapped around it that looped through to the next one—it was an uninterrupted string of sparkles.

The sales associate was ready to put it in a box and let me take it home (he had Babycakes' contact and credit card info), but I wanted Babycakes to go and see it first as I didn't feel right walking out of the store with such an expensive item without running it by him. To that end, we met up later for drinks and dinner and I mentioned to him that I had picked out a necklace, and that it was under $100K. He said he would go and take a look at it (for all he blows money on stupid shit, he also does like getting value for his money).

Babycakes went to see the necklace and he agreed that it was a gorgeous piece. The problem was that the jeweler would not let him take it to an outside appraiser and, because the diamonds had holes in them, Babycakes was convinced that he was being ripped off on the price.

I was annoyed. I did not pick out the necklace because of what it cost. I picked it out because I liked it and because he told me to pick out a necklace.

Babycakes refused to purchase it.

This further annoyed me.

I hadn't asked for a necklace. He told me to pick one out while setting some parameters. I picked one out and then he balked.

A couple of weeks later, we were sitting in our hotel room suite. From my vantage point on the couch, I watched Babycakes bend down on one knee, grab his backpack, and rummage around inside. It was late in the evening, around 9 p.m., and the living room was dimly lit. My stomach dropped when I saw him pull out a velvet box and turn to me, still on one knee.

I have had instances in the past where my sympathetic nervous system has ramped up in response to a stressor, but I do not believe my fight-or-flight system has ever kicked in so decisively—it was all flight. I started to panic, thinking that Babycakes was going to propose to me after four years together. But instead of feeling an overwhelming rush of joy and happiness, my first instinct was to run. That probably should have been my cue to end the relationship, but no. I persisted.

And when Babycakes finally opened the jewelry box,

while my heart beat with the rapidity of a death metal song? It was a diamond necklace, not the one that I had picked out, but one from his jeweler that he brought to see if I liked.

I didn't like it. I wanted the one that I had picked out. And while I unfortunately did not end up with a diamond necklace that evening, I also, fortunately, did not end up with a fiancé.

DAY-TWA

When you are on vacation with your family in Arizona for two weeks over Christmas, sometimes the temptation of online dating is too much to resist. You are in a new geographical region, void of exes, and the possibilities are endless. To that end, I had been active on some dating apps from the day that the plane touched down in the desert.

Now, this may surprise you, but I am very particular about whom I chat with and with whom I agree to go on a date. One man, I will call him Chad, I took an instant liking to. His profile was entertaining, he had a graduate degree, he looked handsome—blond-haired, blue-eyed, with a winning smile and fashionable sense of style. We connected and immediately hit it off. We had a similar sense of humor—mine tends to lean towards the dark and sarcastic—and the text conversation flowed freely. I was situated south, and he was situated north so, after one week of chatting, we agreed to meet at a country club half-way between us to have some drinks.

While I was in the vehicle heading for the club, Chad

texted me: *I'm lost. I'm driving around but can't find the place.*

I asked him to keep me apprised of his travels and was dropped off at the front doors of the club. It was a grand building, with a large, open-air lobby that boasted oversized leather couches and a roaring fireplace. Smartly dressed people milled about; I took a seat in front of the fire and waited for my date.

When Chad walked in, a mere ten minutes later, he flashed me a brilliant white smile. He was outfitted in a sharp navy suit with brown dress shoes. We quickly grabbed a table in the dining area and a waitress brought over some menus.

"How do you feel about champagne?" he asked.

I was fine with some bubbly, so he scanned the menu and ordered a bottle from our server. Despite the time that we had spent texting prior to meeting up, small talk ensued. Things seemed to be going well and I hadn't the faintest clue of what was to come.

After several minutes we got on the topic of a recent trip I had taken to Detroit, whereupon I was robbed of all my belongings. Chad stopped me mid-sentence.

"It's pronounced Day-Twa," he said with a straight-face.

I scrunched up my nose and viewed him through narrowed eyes as I tried to discern whether he was joking.

He was not joking.

"No, it's not," I replied.

"Yes," he insisted. "It's pronounced Day-Twa. It was discovered by a French explorer. I'm from the city," he continued sardonically. "I should know."

"Okay," I said skeptically. "You can call it that, but no one outside of Montreal is going to know what the hell you're talking about."

The waitress came back and set the ice bucket beside

us, popped the cork, and poured us each a glass of champagne. Chad and I clinked glasses and stared at each other while we took a sip.

He set his glass down first.

"You see this suit?" Chad broke the silence and pulled on the jacket lapels for emphasis. "It's bespoke."

I didn't know what to say to this apparent non-sequitur. "Oh?" I raised my eyebrows and took another sip of champagne.

Chad watched as I set my glass down on the table. "How are you feeling?" he asked.

I was thrown off by both Chad's tone and his question. I wasn't sure why, but something in my gut made me feel like there was some kind of sinister undertone to it.

"I feel fine, thanks." I brushed off his question and made a mental note to keep my wits about me.

He stared at me for a second before changing the subject.

"You know, if we start dating, I won't be able to come visit you," Chad said. "You know how you were robbed in Day-Twa? Well, I've been robbed three times, the last time involved a gun and, long story short, I'm not allowed into Canada."

"What?" I asked.

"Yes," he continued. "You know how I live in San Francisco? Well, I have a very extensive and very expensive wine collection. . . you know Jack Ma?" he asked, switching gears. I did know Jack Ma—China's richest man and the founder of Alibaba. I wondered where he was going with this.

"I brought Jack Ma public," he boasted, puffing out his chest with pride.

At this point, all I could think was that Chad was possibly the most full-of-shit man I had ever been on a date with. I'm no finance or business expert, but I do know a fair amount, given my previous partners and my penchant for dating men in the industry. And there was absolutely no way that Chad, in all his bespoke-suit glory, who pronounced Detroit as "Day-Twa," had brought one of the most well-known billionaires in the world public. Despite this, I declined to voice my skepticism and just kept sipping champagne. I was full-steam ahead on the weirdo train at this point, and I wanted to see just where it was going to take me. The conversation became more outlandish as Chad's claims became more outrageous.

After some more unbelievable boasts, Chad ceased bragging about himself and turned his focus towards me: "What are you wearing? Stand up," he commanded.

Bewildered, I did just as he asked. I was wearing a knee-length, empire-waist black dress that was comprised of layers of lace.

"Oh, I see what's going on there. I see what you're trying to do." He gestured to my waist, indicating that I was strategically covering up a fat stomach.

I sat back down, feeling dumbfounded.

"How are you feeling?" Chad asked again as I reached for my champagne.

By this point I was feeling like I was out on one of the strangest dates of my life. But I didn't want to go home. I wanted to see just how weird this guy was going to get.

"I feel fine, thanks," I repeated to him for the fourth time that night.

Chad looked at me and a mischievous smile spread across his face. "You know," he said, lifting his glass to his lips, "I could murder you tonight and bury your body in the desert and no one would ever find you."

He took a drink of his champagne while keeping his eyes trained on my face.

I was speechless.

Chad then set his glass down and adjusted his body in the leather chair, which made a rude sort of sound when his bespoke suit rubbed against the fabric.

He paused.

"I just want you to know, I'm not shitting my pants," he said, looking me in the eye. "That was the chair."

I raised my eyebrows and downed the rest of my champagne. By this time, the bottle was empty and the waitress came over with the bill.

"Where are you two from?" she asked, handing Chad the cheque.

"I'm from Day-Twa," he said smugly.

I stared at the waitress with a "Fuck my life" look on my face while Chad signed for the champagne.

"Did you see what I did there?" he asked after the waitress had walked away.

I did not.

"I gave her a 200% tip," he bragged.

Internally, I rolled my eyes but I agreed to go with him to another bar. This weirdo had piqued my interest, and I wanted to see if I could figure out his deal. Never mind the fact that he had just talked about being banned from my country and burying my body in the desert. It only occurred to me that I may have put myself in danger when the black Uber pulled up and I got inside. I was struck by the notion that maybe he had not actually ordered us an Uber and that this was his murderous accomplice.

I quickly dismissed this idea when Chad began to denigrate the female driver, who was trying to engage us in conversation.

"The *help*," Chad emphasized, staring at the driver in the rearview mirror, "does not speak."

Appalled, I jumped in to defend her. I mean, by this

point I was well aware that Chad was a colossal dickhead. I just hadn't realized how colossal.

When we got to the next bar, which was situated in a broken-down strip mall, I looked around in confusion. It was a strange crowd. The half sports bar, half rock bar, situated between a craft store and a Marshall's, had cheap beer and a jukebox. We had just been served drinks when someone switched the jukebox to "Gimme Shelter" by the Rolling Stones.

Chad turned to me. "I own the rights to this song," he said smugly.

"No, you don't," I said, my voice dripping in disgust. If you're going to lie about something, try to do it in a less egregious, less verifiable manner.

At that point, Chad declared that he was going to marry me, and I watched him walk around the bar, trying to find an ordained minister amongst the crowd. When he failed to find clergy, he told me that we were going to fly to Las Vegas that night and get married. He then called me his "Canadian Queen," went to the jukebox, put on "Oh Canada" and proceeded to sing the Canadian national anthem while standing on top of a stool. The "How are you feeling" questions kept coming at more frequent intervals, and I began to get nervous. I was starting to feel the drinks.

When Chad went to the washroom, I pulled out my phone and discreetly ordered an Uber. I was tipsy, Chad was weird, and it was time to go.

When the Uber pulled up to the bar, Chad was just exiting the washroom. I grabbed my purse, legged it outside, and had just closed the vehicle door when Chad burst out of the bar, looking around for me wildly. I gave him a little wave as the car pulled out of the parking lot and into the night. And while I do believe Chad was a one-off, and I'm not quite sure if I was ever in any danger or merely just out with a master bullshitter, I've sworn off dates on family holidays. I've also taken to correcting people whenever they mention Detroit.

"It's pronounced Day-Twa," I say smugly.

BABYCAKES 13

I have mentioned that Babycakes' lying skills are second to none. This is the man who would deny photographic evidence of a stripper giving him a blowjob. I could have pictures from his own phone, his birthmark prominently featured, being given a blowjob by a stripper, and he would deny that it was him. His dedication to the lie is so bad that it borders on criminal.

This particular morning, Babycakes and I were lying in bed. I was drinking coffee and watching the news while he played around on his phone. While taking a sip of coffee, I happened to glance over at his screen. What did I see? A picture of a scantily-clad woman, striking a seductive pose, sent to him via text message.

Inwardly sighing, I collected myself, glanced back at the television, and then turned my head towards him in full.

"What's that?" I asked in a deceptively innocent voice.

He immediately exited out of the app and switched to his mobile browser.

"Just a picture on Twitter," he lied.

I paused and inwardly sighed again. It looked like this

was going to be a game of cat and mouse. Lie and deny. But what Babycakes didn't know was that I had actually seen the text message itself via my lengthy, inadvertent glance prior to my overt full-head turn.

I scrunched my lips to the side.

"Really?" I asked, voice tinged with a hint of skepticism. "Then why was the picture sent to you in a text message?"

Game, set, and match.

Babycakes missed a beat. He kept his cool, but I could see sweat gathering on his forehead.

"It was from my kids," he lied. "It's a picture of their mom's friend. They sent it to me and said 'she lost so much weight. Look how good she looks.' "

Creepiness factor of a teenager sending his father a seductive photo of his mom's friend aside, a more trusting person, or, perhaps, someone who had spent much less time with Babycakes might have given him the benefit of the doubt. I was less trusting and had spent more time with him.

"Really?" I said, skepticism in full force. "Then you won't have a problem showing me the picture of a text message from your kids with that photo in the conversation?"

At this, he started cursing. "Jesus Christ, this is ridiculous! I'm not going to show you that! This is ridiculous! I'm not going to do it!"

Babycakes had been caught. But instead of having the decency to look ashamed or, better yet, owning up and apologizing, he had chosen to further commit to the lie. Typically, he is a very proficient liar. The man could stand in front of a jury that had him on film running someone over—full face shot with him stating his name, his address, his date of birth, and his mother's maiden name, and he would skillfully and remorselessly lie with enough conviction that it would probably end in an acquittal. After all, *no one* could possibly lie so smoothly, convincingly, and staunchly in such a situation and in the face of such overwhelming evidence. It must have been his twin brother, Maybecakes, who had committed the crime. But in this instance, his lying skills were shamefully sad. I'm attributing it to his hangover, not that that had ever hindered his ability to lie before.

At this point, I couldn't deal with the absurdity of it. I threw on my clothes and headed towards the door with Babycakes in hot pursuit.

"I know you're full of shit," I said to him as I pulled my shoes on. "You know you're full of shit," I continued. "Everyone knows you're full of shit." I put my coat on and reached for the door handle. "I'm not going to sit here and listen to you lie through your teeth. If and when you want to own up to it and explain who the fuck sent you that photo and why, I'll be at home."

I knew who had sent the photo, and I thought that I knew why. Babycakes actually *hadn't* been lying when he told me that it was a photo of his wife's friend. But it was his wife's friend who had sent it, not his son.

Two hours later, I received a phone call. It was from Babycakes.

Did he apologize for lying?

He did not.

"I can't believe I tried to use such a lame lie," he said sheepishly.

To get this straight, Babycakes wasn't sorry that he had lied to me. He was sorry that he hadn't used a better lie.

And yes, I continued to see him.

THE PLAGIARIST

I met Jordan through a friend of a friend. He was kind, had short brown hair, pretty blue eyes, and an easy smile. He was a proud descendant of the British Empire and the circumstances around our first meeting were bizarre, to say the least. I won't go into detail, but they involved the proposition of a threesome with him and his girlfriend. It wasn't something that had ever crossed my mind, but I'm a people person and I am always up for an interesting experience. Which, in this case, meant meeting up for drinks with two people who wanted to sleep with me.

Before getting too far into the story, I will preface it by saying that I did not have a threesome with them. And, in all honesty, I hadn't considered doing so for one second. Mostly I just wanted to see how strange a threesome-proposition meeting would be. I was surprised to find that it didn't actually feel that weird. Really no different than having drinks with friends, albeit with two of them hoping to get you into bed.

We had drinks at a middling, resto-lounge. I got on well

with Jordan and we engaged in animated conversation for the better part of an hour. We really clicked. His girlfriend didn't contribute much to the conversation and seemed miffed, but I had also heard through a friend that she was only dating Jordan because he was wealthy and that she was secretly seeing other people.

After we parted, I let them know that I was flattered that they wanted to include me in their sex life but that it wasn't for me. Jordan asked for my business card and one week later, he called to tell me that he was single.

For the second time in a week, I was flattered. He asked me on a date and we began a courtship that spanned a couple of months. During that time, Jordan was a total gentleman and we spent some great afternoons and evenings sipping wine companionably at nice restaurants. The conversations were engaging, but there was something about Jordan that I found odd. Every time that we were together, he would go off on minutes-long monologues about various subjects. Typically, I wouldn't find it strange—after all, in matters of expertise, it's interesting to listen to individuals share their wealth of knowledge. But with Jordan, his monologues weren't centered around his expertise. Nor were they even original. He was a plagiarist. And he stole all of his material from movies.

On different dates, I caught him quoting from several different films and trying to pass it off as his own. He would sit there, look me in the eye and say: "It's like I always say," and then follow it up with a Tom Cruise monologue taken verbatim from *Jerry Maguire*.

I found it strange but didn't say anything. I could understand if he was a fan of independent films and pilfered their dialogue for self-serving interests. But no— he stole straight from the mainstream. And one *cannot* take a speech straight from *Shrek* and believe that it can be replicated and passed off in public as an original.

How long did it take him to memorize these lines, I wondered? Did he watch certain scenes over and over again, writing the dialogue down and repeating it in front of a mirror to commit it to memory? And how did he decide on what lines he was going to steal? Did he gauge the audience's reaction before making a mental note to look up a certain scene after the movie? Did old dialogue fade when he watched new movies and found more up-to-date or relevant speeches?

One movie that he quoted from with curious frequency was *Religulous*—an early 2000's Bill Maher mockumentary that examines religious beliefs. I'm a fan of Maher—he's a smart and talented comedian. But again—Maher is very mainstream and I couldn't understand how he figured he could get away with it. Was I the only one who noticed, I wondered? Did other people have that little lightbulb moment when hearing Jordan talk? Were others just as confused as I was when they engaged him in conversation? Had anyone ever called him on it? *Maybe so,* I thought, but Jordan just kept going.

In the end, Jordan was a nice guy but he wasn't for me. While I stayed silent about his plagiarism, I knew that my family would not be so kind. I pictured us at a family get-together, with Jordan spouting off lines from a popular movie scene and passing it off as his own:

"It's like I always say," Jordan would boast. "Nobody is gonna hit as hard as life, but it ain't how hard you can hit. It's how hard you can get hit and keep moving forward. It's how much you can take, and keep moving forward. That's how winning is done."

My mom—three Captain Morgans deep at this point, her eyes squinting in a dead giveaway that she was hitting the alcohol point of no return—would turn to him and scrunch up her face sardonically: "Aside from that having nothing to do with Christmas traditions in Europe, Jordan, are you trying to pretend that you actually came up with that quote from *Rocky*?"

I would sit back and watch at this point, waiting for the scene to unfold. When she sensed weakness, my mom could be particularly vicious—like a shark sensing blood in the water. I wasn't sure if Jordan would put up much of a fight, if any, or if he would just hang his head in shame and slink out the door. Knowing what a formidable opponent my mom was, I sensed the slinking would happen in short order, my mom yelling at his retreating back: "It's like I always say, Jordan—if you're not first, you're last!"

BABYCAKES 14

One of the many things that I liked about Babycakes was that, despite being worth nine figures, he wasn't flashy. On a typical day, one in which he is not dressed in a suit, you wouldn't know that he has even twenty dollars to his name. On one of these non-suit days, a chilly winter evening, I showed up at the Ritz to find him decked out in one of the worst outfits I had ever seen: a starched white dress shirt; ripped blue jeans; beat-up sneakers; a vomit-green, shapeless long-rider crafted from the cheapest polyester in creation; a pilling, homemade knit blue scarf; black leather gloves; and a nineties toque from the San Jose Sharks. It looked like a two-year-old had picked out his outfit. Nothing went together. He was a walking Picasso.

I burst out laughing when I saw him and asked what the hell he was wearing, despite finding his lack of give-a-fuck endearing. We headed over to Hooters for drinks and dinner that night, whereupon Babycakes proceeded to spill chili all over his starched white shirt. It was perfect—all that his outfit had been missing was a stain. He was, for all intents and purposes, a literal and figurative mess. A walking, talking, hundred-million-dollar masterpiece.

TROLL AT THE ST. REGIS

For reasons too complicated to get into, I spent a few months living in a luxury hotel. During my time there, I got to know the staff—everyone from the concierge and housekeepers to the bellmen, front-desk clerks, and the bartenders.

Especially the bartenders.

This, however, was in the time of COVID. I hate to even bring it up because I, like I'm sure most everyone else, am so sick of hearing about it. Unfortunately, the militant mask-wearing is integral to this story, but COVID won't be mentioned again.

When I say I was living in a luxury hotel, I mean that I was full-on Anna Delvey—the only difference between the two of us being that she was scamming, although the bill I was left with was *much* lower than what most people would pay. This was owing to a man with whom I was in a "Situationship" and who, thanks to his connections, negotiated a reasonable rate on my behalf.

I had a corner suite on a high floor that consisted of a bedroom with a walk-in bathroom, a living room, wet bar, powder room, entry way, and a workspace. While the room did not allow me to cook any meals, I was provided with a decent-sized mini-fridge that mostly housed salads, hummus, cut veggies, and half-drunk bottles of wine.

It was a curious time to be living in a hotel—I had just moved back to the city after a few months' stint on the other side of North America. I had given up my condo, put all my belongings into storage, and was living like a nomad—albeit a wealthy one. For, again, reasons too long to get into, I had three months before I could start looking for permanent housing, so it was either AirBnb or a hotel.

Cue Mr. Situationship to the rescue.

The staff was friendly and, for a while, I was one of the only guests on the premises. While I knew most of the staffers by name and could recognize them from the eyes up, the bottom half of their faces, obscured by masks, remained a mystery. A certain concierge caught my attention—he was handsome from his dark, black-lashed eyes up: porcelain skin, brooding black eyebrows, and a slash of perfectly-coifed, straight black hair. He also possessed a posh British accent and was a good foot taller than I, even when I was wearing heels.

"Anything I can help you with, Ms. Laboucane?" he would ask when I sauntered by his desk every day. Similarly, he would be there when I walked back through the lobby and would ask me how my day was. I wasn't one hundred percent sure—I know how attentiveness to guests is a part of the concierge job description—but I had a feeling that he was flirting with me. There was nothing overt, no rapid-succession eyebrow raises that might indicate that he had something lascivious on his mind. There was instead a distinct sparkle and warmth that was communicated through his orbs every time we talked. And the more we interacted, the more curious I became—I wondered what was beneath the mask that obscured two thirds of his face.

There was a knock on my hotel door one evening and I peered through the peephole. It was the concierge. He held a silver tray that was bursting with flowers and chocolates. A smile spread across my face: *Flowers and chocolates, how nice!*

My mind immediately went to my Situationship, but the thought vacated my brain almost as quickly as it had entered. The most romantic gift that he had purchased for me to date had been a bottle of Astroglide. Somehow, I doubted that he was choosing a random Tuesday to step up his game. Was it from my parents? I wondered. My sister? Maybe I had a secret admirer? The possibilities were endless.

I opened the door and enthusiastically greeted the concierge: "Hi!"

"Ms. Laboucane," he nodded and then explained that he had brought me a gift as a token for the halfway point of my stay. I was flattered, opened the door wide, and welcomed him in. He walked past me with his impeccable posture, put the chocolates down on the coffee table, and placed the vase full of flowers beside me. Then he straightened, stood there, and smiled—I could tell because of the crinkling at the corners of his eyes.

"Will there be anything else, Ms. Laboucane?" he asked.

I practically swooned.

Yes. There was something else. I wanted him to take off his mask. No. I *needed* him to take off his mask. The curiosity was killing me. I had pictured it over a dozen times, wondering just how handsome the rest of his face would render him.

It was like some low-rent version of *The Phantom of the Opera*. But instead of a theatre, he was haunting my dreams. And, instead of a musical talent, he was adept at getting me whatever I wanted. And I will take a man who can get me a restaurant reservation at the hottest spot in the city or a 4 a.m. snack over a man who is a musical genius any day.

While I felt certain that he was good-looking, I also had visions of him removing the cloth covering and his entire being suddenly morphing into Quasimodo—the facemask somehow hiding a hunchback in addition to the lower half of his face.

"Prior to the pandemic he looked like he belonged under a bridge," I imagined people saying. *"But the mask turned him into a British prince."*

As he stood in my living room, waiting for me to make a request, I couldn't bring myself to ask for what I most wanted. I'm sure there would have been some way for me to teasingly ask him to take off his mask, but I couldn't think that fast and was concerned that I might come off as creepy. Besides, the last thing I needed was to get ousted from the hotel—my home for three months—for being accused of sexually harassing the staff. So, I thanked him, let him know that there was nothing else that I needed, and he left with a flourish after leaving me his card.

Another night, I told myself. I *would* see what he looked like at some point.

I was too optimistic. Unfortunately, before I had the chance to figure out a way to get him to "take it off," as it were, I went out one night and got so shit-faced that I didn't remember getting back to my hotel room. I woke up the next morning feeling shame, regret, and a raging hangover of biblical proportions. You know the kind— where you pass out in bed and rise, three days later. Like Jesus.

I know hotels. The staff talks. And, not knowing if I had crawled to the elevator of my own volition or if the staffers had had to trolley me to my room like a piece of weather-beaten luggage, I couldn't bring myself to hit on him. After all, you can't black out and have hotel staff cart you to your room *and* hit on the hot-from-the-eyebrows-up concierge. I wouldn't want them thinking that I was a *total* disaster.

BABYCAKES 15

One thing that Babycakes really enjoyed was having breakfast at low-brow diners. The trashier, the better. We would sit at the table stocked with ketchup, salt, pepper and tabasco sauce, and Babycakes would order himself up an egg-white omelette the size of his face. He would then proceed to ignore me while he perused that day's newspapers—the *Wall Street Journal* and *National Post*, typically—and sipped his coffee. He sipped a Vodka Caesar if it was a *really* good morning. We were staying at an uptown hotel one chilly winter morning. The previous evening had been one of those rare nights where he hadn't overindulged in the drink too badly and his hangover was nearly non-existent.

In anticipation of his morning meal, Babycakes had taken the liberty of Googling nearby diners the previous evening and determined that our breakfast spot was a mere seven blocks away. Due to the cold weather, however, Babycakes wanted to take the underground walkway. That morning, we ambled through the snow-covered sidewalks outside before reaching the entrance to the underground.

Being an early morning on a workday, the entire underground path was packed full of people, all moving purposefully on their way to work while a smattering of tiny stores hocked their wares.

It was in one of these small stores where Babycakes, walking ahead of me with the single-minded purpose of obtaining his morning newspaper, disappeared. He was there, and then he was not. No bother. I saw the store he had entered, and I pushed my way through the crowd. I finally reached the store and stepped inside, only to find that Babycakes was nowhere to be seen. I looked around, peeking behind stands and scanning the sea of people walking past the store.

Still no Babycakes.

I suddenly realized that, in addition to being down one boyfriend, I was also lost. I was unfamiliar with this section of the underground, having spent next to no time in it. If I am above ground, my navigation skills are second to none. But put me underground with monotonous subway tiles, lack of signage, and a crazy morning rush of commuters, and I am hopeless. I texted Babycakes to see where he was, but quickly realized there was no cellular service in that area. I stood in the midst of the commuters as I searched for any sign indicating directions. Taking a chance, I made a left down a long hallway that I thought might lead me to the outside. Several minutes later, I realized that this hall was not going to lead me to outside and I followed it back to right where I had started. Playing a game of "Eenie, Meenie, Miney, Moe," I selected another path with the same result. Twenty minutes later, I finally emerged outside and the cold air stabbed me in the face like a hundred knives. While I still had not found Babycakes, at least I now had the comfort of knowing where I was. I contemplated for a second, wondering where he could have gone. I figured that there were really only three options: 1. Babycakes was still underground, searching for his lost girlfriend. 2. Babycakes had gone back to the hotel to wait for me. 3. Babycakes had continued on to the diner, unconcerned that he didn't know where I was.

I immediately dismissed option one. And, after a fleeting consideration, dismissed option two. The majority of the things that Babycakes did were self-serving, and I knew that he was hungry that morning. He wouldn't let a little thing like losing his girlfriend stop him from getting his meal.

I started walking in the direction of the diner, which was now several more blocks away due to my underground detour. When I finally saw the diner's sign, I hurried to the front doors, walked inside, and scanned the restaurant. There, sitting at a table on the far left, with a newspaper spread out in front of him, a mug of coffee in his hand, and a half-eaten omelette on a plate in front of him, was Babycakes. I scrunched up my brow, shook my head in exasperation and walked over.

"Hi," I said as he finished taking a drink from his mug.

He looked up at me. "Hi."

"Enjoying your breakfast?"

"Yes, very good, thanks." He took another bite of his omelette and went back to reading his newspaper.

I pulled out a chair and sat down across from him.

"Babycakes, I didn't know where you were," I said as the waitress came over and asked me if I wanted coffee. "I was lost underground. I looked everywhere for you. I didn't know where you were, and I didn't know where I was. Did you even look for me?"

"Eh, you're fine." He brushed me off and adjusted his newspaper. "I figured you would either find your way here or back to the hotel."

I should not have been surprised, but I was. Babycakes, upon discovering that his girlfriend was missing, hadn't even taken a cursory glance around to look for me. He had continued on his way to the diner, found a table, ordered coffee and his breakfast, and proceeded to read the newspaper, completely unconcerned that he had lost me.

I ordered my breakfast and ate it in silence while Babycakes continued to read the news.

He still does not see anything wrong with abandoning me underground that cold winter morning—because "Breakfast is the most important meal of the day."

THE PROFESSOR

I spent a few years working part-time in a lab at the university I attended. It was a fun gig where I was able to learn and participate in cell culturing, mixing reagents, and various experiments. It was a large lab with several Primary Investigators, PIs for short, with adjacent labs on the same floor.

I spotted The Professor one morning when I was on my way to the microscope room. He was tall—6' 2"—with a mop of brown hair that fell loosely around his face in big bouncy curls. His skin was burnt amber, and he had soft, dark eyes. He was on the younger side—somewhere in his early forties, and appeared to be setting up lab equipment.

I knew everyone on my floor, and I had never seen this man before. I learned later that day that his name was Vincenzo, that he was the newest PI, and that his lab would be adjacent to the one that I worked in. According to fellow lab members, Vincenzo had invented a new technique for studying certain types of cells. I was intrigued.

Typically, I would pop by the lab whenever I had

time—between classes, in the evenings, and on weekends, and I saw Vincenzo more frequently. The man seemed to live at his lab, which I kind of understood. Research is integral to academia, so a PI's workspace is of utmost importance.

Our encounters started out as shared eye contact, which morphed into shared smiles, friendly "Hello's," and finally full-on conversations and flirting.

When I was working in the lab during the evenings after most of my coworkers had gone home, Vincenzo would still be there. He would come over to my bench, and we would flirt shamelessly. He would tease me about the classes I was taking, essays I was writing, and the experiments I was running.

It didn't take long before Vincenzo asked me out for dinner. The day happened to be my birthday, and I didn't have any plans. We agreed to meet at a popular Italian restaurant at 9 p.m. the next Wednesday. We had to meet late, he explained, because he had some experiments that he would need to set up for the following day.

At 8:40 p.m. the next Wednesday, I got into an Uber and made my way to the restaurant. It was a large space with tall ceilings and the laughter and chatter of patrons echoed around the room. Vincenzo was seated at a table against a wall, and I slid in beside him. The waitress had already brought menus—everything was written in Italian.

Not being the least bit fluent, Vincenzo assured me he would order a nice vegetarian dish for me. I sat back and happily agreed. While we waited for dinner, we sipped red wine and flirted. Thirty minutes later our meals were placed in front of us—mine, a beautiful-looking ravioli and his, some kind of pasta with meat. We clinked our glasses together, he wished me a happy birthday, and we dug in.

The ravioli was handmade and, as I took my first bite, I

immediately knew something was wrong. It tasted off. I looked at Vincenzo.

"I think this is meat," I said disgustedly, the piece of ravioli still in my mouth. It had been a long time since I had last tasted beef but I did *not* remember it being that gamey.

"Meat?" Vincenzo asked.

"Yes—it's not vegetarian. I can't eat this." I grabbed my napkin and spit out the ravioli.

"Just eat it," he encouraged me.

I could not and did not. I hadn't eaten meat for fifteen years and I wasn't about to start then. I wasn't some sort of fair-weather vegetarian who only cared about the plight of animals until a crispy tray of full-fat bacon was passed around.

The waitress came over to ask us how our meal was, and I explained the mix up. It was not, however, a mistake on the server's part. I discovered that Vincenzo, who was ethnically Italian, who was born and raised in Italy, and who was a native Italian speaker, was apparently not an Italian *reader*. He had ordered me a meat-filled ravioli while assuring me that it was cruelty-free. And it wasn't just your run-of-the-mill beef-filled ravioli. No, no. The ravioli that Vincenzo had ordered me was rabbit. You know—the cute, fluffy, floppy-eared bunnies that people keep as pets. And that some Italians, apparently, feed to unsuspecting vegetarians. I had never even tasted rabbit during my meat-eating years. It was far from the birthday surprise I had been hoping for and, as far as celebratory meals go, it had the distinction of taking the gold medal for worst.

The restaurant closed at 10 p.m. that night and the kitchen was unwilling to make me something new. One thing that the server was able to provide me with, however, was more liquor. So, I sat there and watched Vincenzo eat his dinner as well as mine while I drowned the grumbles in my stomach with wine. We parted ways that evening shortly after ten, when the waitstaff kicked us out. Vincenzo bade me the Italian version of "adieu" and headed off to a straight, men's-only basement bathhouse that he had found on Kijiji.

Happy Birthday to me.

I took an Uber home and passed out on the couch.

BABYCAKES 16

A hallmark of our breakups (of which there were many) was our seeming inability to stay away from one another. It was the weird sort of chase, retreat, chase, retreat pattern that marks those truly toxic relationships. When it's good it's glorious, and when it's bad, it's apocalyptic. When one was committed, the other was not. And the moment that the one who was committed decided that they, too, were out, then the roles would reverse and the flip-flop game of chase would begin.

This particular breakup was instigated by me. I can't recall exactly what triggered it, but between the two of us, we were always finding reasons to part ways. Because I had broken up with Babycakes this time, that meant he was the chaser. And typically, when he was in chase mode, he would use any avenue available to him to try and entice me back. Sometimes it was name-dropping celebrities and inviting me to big events. (I always declined. Celebrities and high-profile events are not the way to my heart.) Other times it was promising me the stability that I craved (building a life together and meeting friends and family).

This time, Babycakes went the money route and tried to impress me with a purchase.

My phone lit up with a text message and photo attachment.

Look what I just bought, the preview said.

I unlocked my phone and clicked on his name. Below his message was a picture of the inside of a private jet.

I rolled my eyes. Babycakes knew that I wasn't impressed by money, yet he still sought to lure me back with the promise of a private plane.

Pausing for a moment, I opened up Google, searched for images, and took a screenshot.

Look what I just bought, I texted back, following up the message with a screenshot of a vibrator.

THAT TIME I UNKNOWINGLY DATED A LIBERIAN WARLORD

Have you ever Googled an ex several years after you dated them? You can be doing something completely innocuous—in my case, applying makeup one Thursday morning—and a man from your past pops into your mind. Before you know it, you put down your makeup brush, pick up your mobile, type in your ex's name and hit "Search."

What do I usually find? A new position in a company, a new business venture, research papers, sometimes a wife, kids, or awards. What, on that Thursday morning, did I find? I found out that I had unknowingly dated a Liberian warlord.

Yes. A fucking Liberian warlord. Accused of heinous crimes against humanity. We are talking murder. We are talking rape. We are talking about atrocious, stomach-turning, horrifying crimes for which he was wanted by international criminal courts.

I remembered reading the banner on my local news station one year previously, which stated that a Liberian warlord, who had been living in the area, had been murdered. I did not click on the article, however; I just read the headline and shook my head in disgust. *How could my country allow a warlord to live here?* Now I was shaking my head in disgust and wondering how I could have dated a warlord and not known it.

I met Bill when I first moved into my building. He was on the shorter side, muscular, and in great shape. We ended up going out for drinks a few times, and he told me all about himself. Unfortunately, he was a low talker, with a heavy accent, so for a decent portion of time I hadn't the faintest idea of what he was saying. Despite that, he managed to convey that he was the son of an African diplomat and, businesswise, he was an importer/exporter who specialized in ice and cocoa. He also had nine cell phones, drove an Escalade, and was typically outfitted in loud, high-end designer clothing. I remember telling my parents about him. They found my description of him to be exceedingly odd and took care to warn me that anyone who had nine cell phones was probably someone with whom I didn't want to spend my time.

In typical form, I brushed aside their concerns and kept seeing him. I remember one instance where we ran into one of my inebriated friends at a club, and my friend started a fight. Bill apologized to me, said that he couldn't get into trouble and high-tailed it out of the venue. There was another instance where we went out for drinks and he drove us home afterwards. A few blocks away from our condo, we were pulled over by the police and Bill began to panic. I remember the look of fear on his face when the police car's lights went off behind us. He had had a couple of drinks over the course of the evening, but not enough to impair him and definitely not enough to account for the way he was shaking before the police officer stepped up to the driver's side door. Another time I met one of his friends, a Southern gentleman who told me about some of their businesses in the USA, which revolved around guns. And while these instances were a bit odd, there wasn't anything about him that I found overly concerning.

We continued to date, taking things slow, but I started to lose interest and, eventually, he got the hint. Over the next few years, I would periodically run into him in the grocery store or in the lobby of our building. Eventually I moved into a new condo and forgot all about him. Until that fateful March morning.

After realizing I had dated such a horrible human being, I immediately turned to Google and devoured every article I could find about him. What I read was ghastly, and it took me a while to come to terms with it. He had seemed like the kindest, gentlest man—soft-spoken and soft-hearted. Someone who was understanding and who helped those who were in need. But the things he was accused of were on the opposite end of the spectrum—they were cruel, inhumane, and grisly. It just goes to show that you never can judge a book by its cover and you never can really know a person. I had experienced this second-hand several times through my love of *Dateline*, but it's a massive shock to the system when it happens to you.

And while Bill was gunned down and died a quick death, I will say, from what I have read, that if what he was accused of is true, he got what he deserved. Although some might argue that his demise was too quick and easy. I can't disagree. After all, the people whom he had a hand in murdering, raping, crucifying, and recruiting as child soldiers had had their lives torn apart and taken away. But maybe a quick death was better than no death at all.

Unsurprisingly, I now take great care to Google my dates beforehand.

THE DOUBLE LIFE

I met Ryan at the infamous hotel in which so many of my stories take place. Stacey, one of my girlfriends, had recently caught her boyfriend cheating. She confronted him and he responded by breaking up with her. I met her at the bar to commiserate over cocktails that same night.

I expected to end up tipsy during the course of the evening, but what I didn't anticipate was meeting someone. Especially because Babycakes was in town, and we were staying at the hotel. So, too, it turned out, was Mr. Someone.

I want to chime in here with a caveat, lest you get the wrong idea. At this time in our relationship, Babycakes and I were "casually dating," which meant that I kept trying to get back together with him, but he kept throwing the term "casually dating" back in my face. Just prior to this night, I had told him about my sister's wedding that was taking place in nine months. "I'm busy that weekend," he had responded without even glancing at his calendar.

Still, I was staying with him and all my things were in "our" hotel room.

Anyway. Stacey, understandably, was in the mood to get lit. She wanted to drown her sorrows and, being an obliging friend, Babycakes and I joined her and her sister for a drink. It was a busy Thursday evening and standing next to the bar was a tall, blond-haired man wearing a suit. He was chatting with another man, also in a suit, who had a ruddy beard. Blondie was attractive, so I turned my attention to him. His name was Ryan, and he introduced himself in a James Bond manner. I mocked him mercilessly for this and then invited him and his friend to join us for the evening.

My girlfriend wanted to go bar-hopping, so Babycakes, Stacey, her sister, Ryan, his friend, and I all headed for a taxi and hit up the city's party district. At the first bar, we did shots. I later found out that Stacey's sister also made out with Babycakes while we were there. *Hello, Red Cross? I'd like to report a disaster: it's my relationship.*

I spent time talking to Ryan and found out that he actually lived in Manhattan and was merely in the city for work. Several shots later, we headed for a bar across the street where we ordered up a round of drinks. Stacey, who was inebriated by now, went around the bar and drunkenly hit on guys. At the same time, I was really hitting it off with Ryan. We seemed to have a lot in common and bantered back-and-forth with glee. At some point, Babycakes realized that he was hammered and had to go back to the hotel. He told me that he was leaving, but I had promised Stacey's sister that I would get Stacey home safely, so I stayed—putting a drunk in charge of a drunk. It turned out okay, but I don't know if it would have been my first choice.

Babycakes went home after saying goodbye to everyone, and I made him promise to leave me a room key in the lobby. He agreed and headed out. He had a conference to attend the next morning and wanted to blunt the inevitable hangover with as much sleep as he could gather at 1 a.m.

I danced with Ryan, kept an eye on my girlfriend, and consumed more liquor until the bartenders announced it was last call. I stuffed Stacey into a cab, and Ryan and I pushed in beside her. We dropped her off at her building before Ryan and I headed back to the hotel.

When I approached the front desk (keep in mind, the staff knew that I was, ostensibly, Babycakes' long-term girlfriend) at 2 a.m. with another man and asked them for the key to Babycakes' room, they informed me that he hadn't left one for me and hadn't given them authorization to give one to me.

I was pissed.

The last thing that I had asked Babycakes to do was to ensure that I had access to our three-day temporary home. Although, given the amount of alcohol he had consumed, I suppose it was understandable that he had forgotten. I asked the front desk to call his room—he didn't answer. I called him from my cell phone—he didn't answer. I texted him—he didn't answer. The bellman went and knocked on his door—he didn't answer. It was unbelievable. The light sleeper who typically bolts awake at a pin-drop was in some sort of alcohol coma that only daylight would relieve. The keys to my condo were in our hotel room, so I couldn't even go back to my place. With deep feelings of annoyance, I announced to Ryan that I would be sleeping in his room for the night.

Ryan didn't seem to mind, and I woke up the next morning—fully clothed and under the covers—to several text messages from Babycakes.

He was pissed. I was pissed.

Regardless, he left a key for me at the front desk before dragging himself to his conference that morning. I gathered my things from the room and went home.

Babycakes and I didn't say much to each other after that. He went home that afternoon and I went to a lounge to meet Ryan. For the past several months, Babycakes had refused my requests to reconcile. Ryan, on the other hand, was keen—we had a great connection and he seemed very sweet.

I went back to Ryan's hotel room that night and, again, slept in my clothing. The next morning, I bid him adieu and he headed back to New York. Ryan and I saw each other again when he was back in Toronto, and we spent the next several months texting each other like teenagers.

Ryan had told me that he was single, had never been married, much less engaged, and that he was waiting for "The One." He teased me about whisking me away to Bora Bora to elope, talked about us having kids, meeting my parents, and moving to Toronto. He showed me pictures of his nephew, gushed about his sister, and told me all about his friends, family, work, and background.

Only, none of it was true. It turned out that Ryan was a grade-A liar. Not only did he have a wife, but he also had two children—one of whom he had passed off as his nephew. I was aghast.

Lying about your wife is one thing, but lying about your children is a betrayal. Sure, Babycakes lied—with impunity—but he would never lie about his own kids.

Ryan's and my liaison ended with me contacting his wife. He begged me to keep it a secret, but I declined. If the shoe had been on the other foot, I mused, I would have wanted all the information about my cheating spouse. I told her everything. And I told myself that revenge had nothing to do with it.

BABYCAKES 17

On our way home from the piano bar one December night, Babycakes and I drunkenly got into the hotel elevator and pressed the number for our floor. Halfway up, the elevator stopped and the doors opened into a loud, music-filled lobby. Two people dressed in cocktail clothing stepped onto the lift, and Babycakes and I looked at each other and promptly stepped off.

The lights were dimmed and music was pulsating from two large doors to the left of the lobby. It sounded like a party, and we were both dressed up and in the mood, so into the room we waltzed.

It wasn't that large of a crowd, maybe forty or fifty people at most, and clearly a company celebration. Babycakes headed for the bar while I headed for the dance floor, discarding my shoes before joining in the fun. Minutes later, a bottle was thrust into my hand. A jovial Babycakes clinked his Stella Artois against mine, and we took over the dance floor while people gave us sidelong looks. We didn't look out of place because we were both dressed for a party, but there was something about us that stood out—possibly the fact that no one in the room had seen either of us before that night. And, despite the flowing drinks and the late hour, I figured it was really only a matter of time until we were found out. So, we made the most of our time, tearing up the dance floor with wild abandon before hitting up the bar for another round of beer.

It was on my way back to the dance floor that I spotted a woman in her late sixties sitting at a table alone, watching people dancing. She had gray hair and was wearing a long, black chiffon dress. Wanting to include everyone in the fun, I danced over and tried to coax her into joining us. She smiled politely and resisted, so I danced back over to Babycakes. I glanced back at the older lady moments later and saw a brunette in a knee-length sheath dress talking to her intently. They were looking our way. Moments later, the brunette walked over to us with a stern look on her face.

"This is a private party," she said aggressively.

"Oh?" Babycakes and I looked at each other innocently like we had no idea that we had stumbled into a private party. As if a party had somehow spontaneously erupted around us.

"Yes. That woman," she pointed to the older lady whom I had tried to coax onto the dance floor, "is the owner of the company."

In trying to spread a bit of Christmas cheer, it seemed that I had landed myself on the naughty list.

"You have to leave," the brunette ended firmly.

"Oh, okay," I smiled. "Thank you for letting us join!" I thanked her, ignoring the fact that we hadn't been invited nor had we asked to join. "We had a great time!"

She stared at us as I turned, grabbed my shoes and Babycakes' hand and headed for the elevator.

"Fuck, that was fun!" Babycakes continued to dance in the elevator as it rose to our floor. We arrived at our room and I proceeded to order snacks: it was 1 a.m. and carbs were calling. No sooner had I hung up the phone with private dining and turned around than I saw Babycakes lying on the floor. He was curled up on the carpet in the fetal position, wearing nothing but his underwear. His clothes were strewn around him. Babycakes, apparently, was spent.

After an unsuccessful attempt to rouse him from his stupor, I left him there while room service wheeled in our table full of fries and grilled cheese sandwiches. The employee was clearly a seasoned staffer. He did not even blink at seeing a nearly nude man passed out on the floor. After some French fries and a grilled cheese sandwich, I packed it in and went to bed.

The next morning, I woke up in the epicentre of a potato explosion. I rolled over and discovered that stale French fries were strewn about the sheets. It appeared that Babycakes had woken up at some point during the night, grabbed the *pomme frites*, crawled into bed and had a field day—spilling the basket in the bedding and passing out on top of it.

He woke up a little while later, greatly confused as to what was stabbing him in his back and, upon discovering the source, shook his head, popped a stale French fry in his mouth, and groaned in self-judgment.

THE "INTERNATIONAL ARMS DEALER"

True to form—as is probably evident by now, I have a habit of doing the same thing over and over again and ending up with similar results—I met Shiv on Bumble. He was visiting from New York City and his first photo showed him in a suit, with his black hair smartly parted and a winning smile on his tan-skinned face. I saw that he was 5' 8", which is several inches below my usual cut-off, but no matter—he was a dapper dresser with a winning smile and apparently possessed an accent.

I was sold.

Besides, maybe he had extra inches where it mattered.

I showed up at the lobby bar of his hotel, grabbed a seat and a drink and waited. And waited. And waited. Shiv, it turns out, was uptown meeting with a client. Forty-five minutes later he arrived, a bit chunkier than he had appeared in his pictures, but charming and smartly dressed. He apologized profusely and took a seat. Pleasantries were exchanged with more sprinkles of apologies, and then Shiv regaled me with tales of his travels throughout the USA. Born and raised in the UK but working out of an office in

NYC, he had been taking advantage of his time in the United States to travel the country. When he spoke about his first time at a rodeo, he stood up, acted out his story, and started speaking like he was from the Deep South. Picture this—a short, stocky Indian man in a sharp suit bastardizing his British accent with a poorly-imitated Southern twang while walking around like he's John Wayne.

We were in a nice lounge and people were staring.

Despite his rodeo story, Shiv really was the personification of posh. Because of that, after our first drink, I brought him to a college bar, one where the beer is cheap and plentiful, and the patrons are drunk and underaged. In addition to this, the floor was sticky, the tables were grimy, and the place smelled of stale beer.

It was perfect.

We stuck out like sore thumbs in the place, both dressed up in corporate clothes while drunken twenty-two-year-olds stumbled around us. We ordered a pitcher of beer— the Brit capitulating and giving up his posh drink for my preferred Coors Light. Shiv and I laughed as we watched the college kids dancing, making out, and generally making asses of themselves. There wasn't a lot of talking, given the volume of the music, but there was a fair amount of yelling in a desperate attempt to communicate. After about an hour of this I was tired and we were going to head out—a quarter of the beer was still left in our pitcher. When one of the college students saw us putting our coats on, he staggered over to the table and asked us if he could have the rest of our beer.

The image of my posh British date in his suit, with his hair perfectly coifed and his finishing-school manners, being asked by a drunken college kid if he can finish off our pitcher of beer is one that I will never forget. We told the kid that he was welcome to the beer, but that he would have to get another glass. The kid thanked us, grabbed the pitcher, and proceeded to drink directly from it. Apparently, he wouldn't have to get his own glass.

Shiv tried to get me to go home with him that night but I declined, and he left the city early the next day. I'd questioned him about his job specifics, being curious about what he did for a living, but he had been evasive. He told me that he didn't want to get into it, and we didn't. I wasn't sold on him, but I had enjoyed our time together and was open to seeing him again the next time that he was in the city, so we made plans.

The next time he was in town, we started off with drinks in a lobby lounge and then headed over to one of my favorite restaurants for dinner. When the appetizers came, our talk turned to his career.

"I didn't want to tell you before," he said seriously. "I wanted to make sure that I could trust you. I'm actually an international arms dealer." He followed that up with some vague details about a deal he was doing in the Middle East that revolved around some weapons technology.

Remember how I stated a few sentences ago that I wasn't really that sold on Shiv? After finding out that he was an international arms dealer, I was *really* into him.

I found out two months later that he was totally full of shit and actually ran a pension fund, but thinking that he dealt in international arms was fun while it lasted. It also made me pause and consider, however briefly, that my measure of a potential mate might need some serious recalibration.

THE DINNER OF SHAME

Despite discovering that Shiv was full of shit, I enjoyed his company and we did see each other a few times after that. One of these times we met for dinner. He had a two-hour stopover in my city before heading home and we met for an early meal. It had been a couple of years since we had seen each other and I was in a "Situationship" with Brent. I showed up at the restaurant—a fine-dining establishment that I liked—before Shiv. For several reasons but mostly due to being so busy with work that I had forgotten, I realized after I was seated that I hadn't eaten all day.

No bother. I ordered a glass of wine and waited for my date.

Shiv showed up twenty minutes later, and we quickly placed our orders, which included two glasses of wine. Shiv would have to leave before we finished dinner, he regretfully informed me. His plane had been late landing and, due to his departing flight home and the traffic, he could only stay for thirty minutes.

I had started on my second glass of vino before our main course arrived, and I could feel the alcohol go to my head. I was on a liquid diet at this point and to blunt the effects I had ordered pasta, hoping that the carbs would soak up the delectable poison sloshing around in my stomach.

When Shiv announced apologetically that he had to leave, having only made his way through one half of his meal, he kissed me on the cheek and suggested that I stay and enjoy my dinner.

It was a cute gesture and one that I happily accepted. Shiv motioned for the waiter, ordered me another glass of wine, signed for the cheque and then left. I sat there enjoying the pasta, the wine, and the ambience. After I finished my meal, I headed for the bathroom and debated having one more glass of wine before I headed for home.

I felt tipsy, but not over-the-top tipsy. This, however, was owing to the fact that, while I had consumed three glasses of wine in the span of one hour and fifteen minutes, the full effects had not yet hit my bloodstream.

I stared at myself in the bathroom mirror. I looked good. I had dressed up for my date, and it would be a shame to waste all that effort.

Decision made, I saddled up to the bar. Two people sat a couple of chairs down from me and, aside from that, the restaurant was sparsely populated. I ordered a glass of wine and started talking to the bartender. Her name was Crystal and she was an engaging sort.

As I watched her pour out my glass, the glasses previous caught up to me like something out of *A Christmas Carol*. But it was the Ghost of Liquor Past—and that "past" was ten minutes ago. Unfortunately, the Ghost of Liquor Past brought the Ghost of Dating Present—Mr. Situationship. Not him physically, by any means, but the alcohol-fueled yearning. This led to me bitching and moaning to Crystal about Mr. Situationship and showing her pictures. At some point the owner of the restaurant came over and I started chatting with him as well as the two gentlemen at the bar.

And then I woke up in my bed. Alone. With a massive hangover. Despite wearing four-inch high heels, I had somehow navigated my way home without breaking a bone, sustaining a cut, or losing any of the contents of my purse. Dignity was a different matter, but in order to lose that, I reasoned, you have to have possessed it in the first place.

I digress.

I excluded myself from that particular restaurant for two months afterwards out of shame. Like some sort of gambling addict. *At least* they *could remember what had brought them to the point of exclusion in the first place,* I thought uncharitably. For all I knew, I had hit on my bar mates, knocked over a chair, thrown up on the floor, and crawled home.

Fast forward two months later and Mr. Situationship suggested that we go out for dinner. He liked the restaurant that I had banned myself from and I hadn't confessed to him the reason that I refused to go. That night, I relented. We couldn't agree on a restaurant, and it was a Thursday. The place would be packed.

We walked in and, as expected, there were people everywhere. We took a table in the dining room a little away from everyone and ordered drinks. Ten minutes later a man walked over. I recognized him. It was the owner of the restaurant. The owner who, in all likelihood, had watched me crawl out of his establishment on my hands and knees two months before. He made eye contact with me, and he made eye contact with my date, who greeted the owner like a long-lost friend.

Because, it turned out, he was one.

I saw the barely-concealed look of amusement on the owner's face as my date introduced me. If I had any doubt that he remembered me, it was dashed by the glint in his eye and knowing smirk playing around his mouth. He remembered me. And he definitely remembered me drunkenly bitching about the man who was currently seated across from me.

The moral of this story? Don't drink and whine. And definitely don't do it on an empty stomach. Or at least, don't do it in your own neighborhood.

BABYCAKES 18

There was, as I noted earlier, a sizeable age gap between Babycakes and me. It was all the more noticeable because I have a bit of a baby face. It wasn't something that we thought about often, but there were instances when it was brought to our attention. Like one night when we attended an NBA game.

It was a chilly winter evening, and we were standing in line outside. Babycakes was in a black suit and black cashmere coat and I was in high heels, a mini-dress, and a thigh-length winter jacket. The line to get in was long, and we were about ten people back from the front of the queue. Directly in front of us was a middle-aged man and his wife. No one was happy about being forced to wait outside in the cold, slow-moving queue, and patience was in short supply. I don't remember who bumped into whom first, but soon words were flying between Babycakes and the middle-aged man. The two men lobbed insults back and forth as the wife and I awkwardly stood by, staring at our partners, who were working to one-up each other on the denigration front. I thought Babycakes had gotten the upper hand when the man, with one final sneer, said "Yeah, enjoy watching the game with your daughter!"

Touché.

I laughed my ass off. Babycakes, however, saw red.

By this time, the couple had just put their items through the x-ray machine and stepped through the metal detector. Babycakes waited until we had done the same, before he began scanning the crowd, vowing to go and find the man and "kick his ass."

I had to physically hold him back—no easy feat when you're dealing with a 6' 1", inebriated man who holds himself in high esteem and is generally looking for a fight. And while I agreed that the man in front of us had, indeed, been a massive dick, I also had to admit that, when it came to his last comment, he had a point.

MIKE

I met Mike through work. He was a few years younger than I, a medical student, and we were working on separate projects for the same physician. During a Christmas lunch, in which the doctor brought together those who had collaborated on different projects, we ended up seated next to each other. Mike was not my typical type. He had dark puppy-dog eyes, a prominent nose, toasted skin, and short, almost-shaved brown hair. He was Arabic and had a dark, sarcastic wit that forged an instant connection between us. Before the end of the meal, we exchanged numbers and began texting. His sardonic humor spilled over to SMS, and we began a sporadic texting relationship that spanned several months.

That summer, Mike, who was a teetotaler with a strong faith in God, suggested that we meet for drinks. We made plans to meet on a patio one Friday afternoon and I arrived to find him already seated at the corner of the bar.

No sooner had a glass of water been placed in front of me than I turned to my companion and watched as a seagull flew overhead and shit on his shirt. Directly on his left shoulder. And we're not talking just a little bit of bird shit. We are talking a *lot* of bird shit.

Mike failed to notice and, not wanting to embarrass him five minutes into our first date, I "failed" to tell him.

At the same time, I couldn't stop myself from staring. We had one drink and then headed inside the restaurant. Lower lighting, I told myself, would mask the stark-white bird shit that practically glowed on his navy dress shirt when we were seated outside.

Our rapport was unparalleled, but the lower lighting did nothing to mask the excrement. At one point, Mike excused himself to go to the washroom. I assumed that when he was in there, he would see the stain on his shirt, clean it off, and I would then be able to stop staring.

He did not, apparently, see the stain on his shirt, and after he sat back down and we continued our conversation, I struggled to keep my eyes fixed on his face.

Despite his looking like a pigeon's roost, Mike's and my conversation was electric. His intelligence was a turn-on, we shared similar values, and we had tons to talk about. By the end of the evening, several glasses of wine (for me) later, I definitely had a buzz on.

We left the restaurant and Mike offered to drive me home. I accepted and we headed for the car park. It was late and the poorly lit parking lot was dark and shadowy. When we reached the door that led to the stairs, Mike suddenly pushed me up against the concrete wall in a darkened corner. His lips were immediately on mine and he pressed his body close as he kissed me with unbridled passion. He was aggressive, but I was kind of into it—after all, we had an undeniable connection. Still, I was acutely aware of the closeness of his bird-shit shoulder, and I didn't want it rubbing off on my clothes.

Minutes later, a family happened by and I took their

appearance as my cue to escape. I thanked Mike as I hurried away and legged it for the street, where I stepped into a cab.

I saw Mike a few times after that, and I really believe that we could have had something—but there was something about him that I didn't entirely trust. The best summers of his life, he had told me, involved working on a farm where he would coax baby animals into his arms and then use a knife to slit their throats.

I've referenced *Dateline* at least once in this book, and Mike's favorite summer pastime of slaughtering baby animals set off some Keith Morrison red flags. If Mike was able to play Judas to such innocent, angelic creatures and enjoy it, what could he do to me?

I never gave it a chance to find out, and he eventually moved across the country for residency. It's a bit frightening to know that this man, who could betray innocent creatures and enjoy it, is now a physician. A surgeon, I could understand, given their typical cold and callous nature. But no—Mike is a family doctor.

MR. SITUATIONSHIP 1

We met on Bumble. Matched and exchanged a few messages, which tapered off until he drunkenly spotted me on a downtown patio one evening and messaged me. A few weeks later, we met in person. I found Brent to be handsome, and our conversation was comfortable and fun. That evening we parted ways with an awkward goodbye. There were no "Thank you's", hugs or pleasantries on his part. As if there was an invisible barrier between us, Brent stood five feet away from me and said, "Bye."

I assumed that Brent just wasn't that into me, but the next day he passively said to let him know if I wanted to get together again. I thanked him for our drinks the previous evening and happily agreed.

The next time we went out was where things began to get interesting. Sitting at the bar, ten minutes into our second date, he confessed that he had "done everything sexually you can think of." This was simultaneously curiosity-piquing and off-putting. "Everything sexual" that I could think of was vast—I do, after all, have access to the

Internet. At the same time, what would possess a man to reveal this to someone on a second date after the first date had appeared to end in indifference? Was he trying to impress me? Shock me? Gauge where I stood on the spectrum of sexual achievements?

The red flags were flying high, but this was one flag that both intrigued and repulsed me. What was he into sexually? Things that I hesitate to even put into words. I have been pretty vanilla for most of my sexual life but Brent was the polar opposite. He was dominant in every sense of the word. He searched out and coveted every depraved sexual act one could think of. I had heard of BDSM before, of course, but had never dabbled. Brent changed that. Drastically. He would leave bruises on my body that would take weeks to go away, and soon he started disclosing sexual acts that he wanted me to participate in. *I want to piss on you,* he wrote in a text.

Ew. The corners of my mouth turned down and I grimaced in disgust. But I didn't say no. Instead, a frightening thing happened: any new sexual act that he mentioned he wanted me to try would result in immediate revulsion, followed by a four-day period of quiet consideration, which would then turn into active interest and an overwhelming desire to please him. It's a scary thing to discover this about yourself, and before I knew it, I was five drinks deep and being pissed on.

Now, I liked Brent. Like, *really* liked him. And probably not in spite of him being quite possibly the most emotionally-unavailable man on the planet, but most likely because of it. He was fun, handsome, successful, great in bed, and intelligent. He was also cold, emotionally closed off, and could be a massive, *massive* dickhead.

He wielded sex as a weapon and would withhold it if I did or said something that he found displeasing. Similarly, he would subject me to the silent treatment to manipulate me into doing what he wanted. We regularly had explosive arguments that culminated in him yelling and me in tears. Sometimes these arguments were in private. Most times these arguments were in public—started in restaurants and spilled out onto sidewalks. We were *that* couple. We weren't just a dumpster fire. We were the Staten Island dump.

Despite this, I continued to date Brent and was subjected to his increasingly bad behavior. He did have his positive qualities, and I don't discount that I was equally to blame by continually allowing him to be a part of my life, but Brent was a total twat towards me for the most part—lying, taking days to respond to my texts, canceling plans at the last minute, refusing any forms of affection, eschewing a relationship or commitment but pushing for anal sex and threesomes. There was one instance, however, where he was the unintended architect of his own payback.

Brent came over one afternoon for drinks, snacks, and golf. He pointed out the golfers on T.V. and provided running commentary on each of them as we sipped companionably and picked at the snacks. One hour in, I set my wine glass down, undid his shorts, opened my mouth, and went to town. During this time, he took the opportunity to aggressively slam my head down and force himself down my throat to the point of tears and gagging. Afterwards, we lay on the couch together watching T.V. and talking.

Several minutes later, Brent, still naked from the waist down, sat up, looked at his genitals, and let out a panicked "What the fuck!"

Perplexed, I followed his gaze down to his penis where bright-red blood was pouring out of the opening. And I'm not talking just a little bit of blood. It was *a lot* of blood. All of it bright red, which meant it was fresh and potentially serious. Additionally, having never heard of an instance where blood started haphazardly pouring out of a man's penis, I was pretty sure that this was bad. We were going to have to go to the emergency room.

I pictured Brent and I in the waiting room at the ER, him with a wad of gauze pressed to his crotch while everyone stared at us in curiosity. Complicating matters was Brent's aversion to using the proper terminology for anything genital-related. He corrected me any time I used the words vagina, labia, penis, or testicles. "It's pussy, lips, cock, and balls," he would state aggressively. I imagined us in the examination room, with the physician asking Brent about his symptoms.

"Is it on the tip of your penis?" the physician would ask.

"I believe you mean my cock, Doctor," Brent would correct him. "It is on the tip of my cock."

A power struggle would ensue, with Brent stubbornly trying to force the physician to use his filthy language, while refusing to elaborate on his problem, until the doctor capitulated. I was looking forward to our trip to the ER at this point.

I ran to the bathroom and grabbed some wet wipes and after Brent wiped himself off, we examined his penis more closely. The blood kept coming, but a light bulb suddenly went off. Brent did not have a sudden onset of testicular cancer, nor was he bleeding internally. Nor, sadly, were we going to have to go to the hospital.

Brent was bleeding from my blow job.

It really spoke to my oral sex skills. Although it turned out that it was actually Brent's fault—he was a little too aggressive when it came to forcing down my face, and one of my molars had paid him back in kind. In trying to punish me, he had actually punished himself. It was poetic justice of the penis. Or, in Brent's case, poetic justice of the cock. And every time he peed for several days after that he had a painful reminder of me that somehow felt very fitting.

BABYCAKES 19

One instance that should have clued me in to where I stood in Babycakes' life was one day when we were sitting at the bar at the Ritz. This was prior to the popularity of WhatsApp and when straight-up text messaging was the way to go. I thought that it would be cute to text him while he was sitting next to me, engrossed in a conversation with the bartender. So, I did.

His phone lit up, he looked down at it, looked at me, and then I, too, looked at his screen. The text that I sent him had gone through, but there was something odd about it. Instead of showing that it came from me, his ostensible girlfriend, his screen said that it was from someone named "Guy Savard." I looked at him and pointedly asked why he had apparently saved my phone number under the name "Guy Savard."

It was an accident, he claimed. Honest mistake. Could have happened to anyone. Never mind the fact that we had been dating for six months by this point, and I looked nothing like any of the ancient and balding Guy Savards on Google.

I imagined Babycakes, the staunch Republican, sitting amongst a group of guys with his phone on the bar in front of him, and a text message popping up from "Guy Savard": *Come do me, Babycakes. I want you inside of me.*

"What's that?" one of his friends would ask in horror.

"Wrong number," Babycakes would claim while hastily snatching up his phone.

It was almost enough to make me laugh. Almost.

He quickly changed my name in his contacts list, but kept it to my first initial and last name. I know. Not suspicious in the least. After this, if he had been particularly badly behaved, I would occasionally refer to myself as "Guy Savard" during shopping trips—as in, "Guy Savard wants one in every color."

THE CURRENCY TRADER

I mentioned in a previous chapter that I spent several months living in a luxury hotel. It's always interesting the people you meet when sitting in hotel lobbies, restaurants, and lounges. It's very nomadic.

My suite did not have a kitchen, so most of my meals were either ordered in, delivered via room service, or ordered from the upstairs restaurant and lounge. I fell into a bit of a routine during my time there; if I felt like going upstairs, I would sit at the bar and have a glass of wine while I waited for my dinner. I always took it to go and would sometimes stay for an extra drink if there was someone interesting to talk to, or if the bartenders weren't overly busy.

One night I popped upstairs just after breaking things off with Mr. Situationship. I had had a couple of drinks and was about to order dinner to take the edge off. For some reason, I have always struggled with the notion of fortifying my stomach with food *before* having drinks. It only ever occurs to me after a few cocktails that I really should have eaten. This typically results in my B.A.C hovering in the high one hundreds.

I flounced up to the bar and found a chair on the far left. It was a busy Thursday night, and there was a couple seated to my right and a fashionably-dressed gentleman seated to my left. The bartenders were busy but pushed a beer in front of me before I even sat down. I ordered risotto to go and then pulled out my phone and began dead-scrolling Instagram.

"What would we do without our phones?" came the voice of the well-dressed man seated next to me.

I turned and smiled: "Probably talk to people sitting next to us at the bar."

From there began a two-hour conversation with Jason. He was slender, silvery-blond, and wearing red slacks and a crisp, patterned button-up shirt. During the day, he was a currency trader who lived in Manhattan. By night, he was a D.J., and he had flown in for a gig the day before. His night-time career left him in my city often, he said, and he always stayed at this hotel. We shared an animated conversation about our careers, our pasts, futures, and our presents and had two drinks together before calling it a night. When the elevator stopped on my floor, Jason followed me off.

"Can I get your number?" he asked.

I happily rattled it off.

Playful smirks danced on both our faces as we stood there and gazed into each other's eyes.

"It was lovely to meet you, Jason." I took a step back, still smirking. "Have a good night."

I left Jason at the elevator banks and headed for my room with my now-cold risotto in tow.

Over the next few months, we exchanged periodic text messages. Tentative plans were scheduled on different dates, but inevitably all were cancelled. Finally, one day in late July, Jason texted and asked that I pencil him in for mid-August.

I will be there for certain this time, his text message read. *I'm coming for two nights for personal reasons.* By this time, I had almost forgotten what Jason looked like. But I remembered that we had a great conversation, so I blocked off the dates in my calendar.

The day that Jason was slated to arrive rolled around quickly, and at 6 p.m. the evening before I received a text from him. *I'm here a night early,* it read. *It's last-minute, but do you want to get together tonight?*

I was game and asked for an hour to get ready. We met for drinks at the hotel bar where we had first met. Our conversation flowed as easily as it had that first night, and we soon moved onto another location; we stayed there until they shut the place down. Jason walked me home, and we kissed before parting ways with a promise to see each other the next night. We planned to meet for drinks at the Ritz.

I was massively hungover the next day as I had consumed a non-negligible amount of wine the night before. Somehow, I managed to make myself look presentable and staggered out the door that evening to meet Jason. He had secured a table outside, and we stayed for one drink before making our way over to one of my favorite lounges. It's a small space that is done up in dark wood tones, with furniture that evokes old English aristocracy. We cozied up on a couch and the waitress brought us drinks while we chatted.

The conversation took a turn when Jason suddenly interjected: "I asked the hotel staff about you," he said casually.

I was dumbstruck and didn't quite understand what he meant.

"What?" I asked

"The hotel," he said. "Where we first met. I went there today and asked the staff about you. The doormen, concierge, front-desk staff, and the bartenders. The bartenders told me *a lot* about you."

I felt violated. *Why would he do that?*

Jason relayed that he didn't know my deal and so he had decided to ask around. Instead of, you know, asking me and getting it straight from the source. I might be a high-class call girl, he mused. Or maybe I actually lived at the hotel and had a husband whom I was cheating on.

I was once again struck dumb.

I can understand being wary of someone when you first meet them—there are a lot of scammers and shady people out there. But going behind someone's back to get dirt on them and then positing that they might be a prostitute or a cheater? It was a weird second date. Why would he not just Google me like everyone else?

"I don't know what anyone told you," I replied. "But I'm not a call girl, nor do I have a husband. I don't know what else to tell you."

Jason took a sip of his drink.

"What was the story one of the doormen told me about then?" he asked. "Something about you kissing a man in the lobby."

I was confused. I hadn't kissed anyone in the lobby and racked my brain trying to figure out what he could possibly be talking about. I had nothing to hide, and I knew the doormen well so I couldn't see them mixing me up with some other woman. The only thing that I could think of was a night two months prior, when I had allowed a man to buy me a drink at the hotel bar and then left shortly after.

The man decided to leave at the same time as me, and when we got outside, I thanked him for the drink and he tried to stick his tongue down my throat in response. It was not welcome, and I managed to dodge it. His lips didn't even graze my cheek.

"The doorman saw you get into a taxi with him," Jason said.

I scrunched up my brow.

"No, he didn't. I didn't get into a taxi with anyone, so I don't know where he's getting that from."

Jason took a long sip of his drink and set the glass down with a thud.

He stared at me for a moment.

"I didn't actually ask any of the staff about you," he said smoothly. "I just wanted to see if you would confess to anything."

I was incredulous. What kind of psycho makes up a story to try and get you to confess to something? *A manipulative psycho.*

"I just want to make sure that you are who you say you are. And that you're not offering 'The Girlfriend Experience' and that you're not married or a prostitute."

It was absurd. I was actually having a conversation with someone, on a date no less, who had spent a considerable amount of time calculating the probability of me being a prostitute. And "The Girlfriend Experience?" What the hell was that?

I was thoroughly put off, having cycled through a vast array of emotions in a very short timeframe. None of them were good.

Jason walked me back to my place and, before we parted, he stared deep into my eyes.

"I love you," he said, still staring.

I stared back and pretended I didn't hear him.

Less than one hour ago this man had been questioning me and my motives and had pulled some crazy manipulation tactics to dig for dirt. Was I an escort? Did I provide "The Girlfriend Experience?" Was I a high-class hooker? Now he was telling me that he loved me. On our second date.

Jason flew back to Manhattan and we never saw each other again. He texted me a few times, but we never met up. I wish I could say that I've stopped befriending strangers in hotel bars and going on dates with them, but I haven't.

Now that I think about it, it kind of sounds like something a prostitute would do. Maybe Jason was onto something.

MR. SITUATIONSHIP 2

Brent and I had been dating for a while, but for six months we were long distance. I moved away, but we kept in contact by texting, sending photos, talking on the phone, and sexting. I was lying in bed one morning, massively hungover from the night before, when a notification pinged on my phone. It was a text message. From Brent.

Send me a photo of you sticking your tongue out, it read.

No pleasantries, no small talk. Brent was in the mood, and he wanted nudes.

Can't, I texted back. *Will send tomorrow if I am still alive.*
Still alive?

I went on to explain my post-liquor predicament, texting with one eye closed because the faint light from the phone hurt my eyes.

Come on, he urged me. *Be a good girl and send a photo.*

Grimacing, I clicked the camera app on my phone, turned it to "selfie" mode and snapped a picture. The resulting photo may as well have been a paint swatch for Sherwin Williams' Blackout. The room was pitch black and so was the picture. I sent it to Brent and received a heavily-frowning emoji in reply.

The next day, I felt like a new person. My headache had abated, and seventeen hours of sleep had done wonders for my complexion. I hadn't forgotten about Brent's request, and I snapped some sexy photos of me with my tongue out. I chose the best one, cropped it, and sent it to him. The gray "read" checkmarks quickly turned to blue and Brent began typing. I exited out of the app and a message from Brent popped up on my screen.

Good first try.

I reread the message.

Good first try.

I was dumbfounded. I had expected enthusiasm for the sexy selfie that he had specifically requested. Instead, I received a participation trophy for my efforts. The photo was, apparently, so bad that he couldn't even muster up the energy to put an exclamation mark at the end of the sentence. I was the Miss Congeniality of nudes.

A few weeks later, Brent requested a sexy photo. I was wary and debated the merits of spending all afternoon trying to perfect my pose, and the probability of the picture going over as intended. My humiliation at being told *Good first try* would be magnified tenfold if it happened again—I realized I might never recover. I could see the *New York Post* headline in my mind: "Woman so Traumatized by Man's Response to Nudes She Vows Never to Send One Again."

I spent a few more minutes debating my response and then a thought popped into my head. I had a solution for the sexy selfies. A solution that would both spare my dignity and give Brent what he wanted.

I texted him back.

How about you just send me some nudes that you like and I'll

Photoshop in my face?

BABYCAKES 20

Babycakes and I were fighting one Thursday. About what, I can't recall, but I know it was bad. It was also before I discovered the magic of compromise and communication through therapy. Back then, ignoring the individual and leaving the scene was how I typically dealt with things. In this instance, I left Babycakes in the lobby of a shopping mall and headed home in a huff. Productive? No. Satisfying? Yes.

We were at the point in our relationship where Babycakes would no longer chase me. Instead, he would saddle up to a bar and drink himself into a stupor before engaging me in an all-night antagonistic texting war.

We had fought early in the evening, and I was regretting my decision. I didn't actually *want* to spend the night alone. I just didn't know how to appropriately communicate my displeasure and had instead legged it home. Our ensuing back-and-forth text battle consisted of me apologizing and trying to convince Babycakes to come to my place. This was, of course, interspersed with impulsive, passive-aggressive texts. It took the better part of an hour, but eventually Babycakes relented and got into a cab.

When he showed up on my doorstep, he was swaying. Despite only being apart for approximately two hours, Babycakes had gotten lit. Never one to turn to water, when I asked him what he wanted to drink, he requested vodka.

I gave him a skeptical look but poured him a stiff drink and watched as he chugged it back in earnest. I said nothing but I couldn't help feel that I had played no small part in driving him to it.

I poured him another glass, and we took a seat on the couch while I launched into what I thought was a very humble and heartfelt apology. I apologized for our fight earlier and apologized for my behavior—I was immature sometimes. Instead of pausing, thinking, and then acting, I was more prone to overreacting. Ten minutes in, I noticed Babycakes' eyes glaze over. Like icing on a donut. It occurred to me then that Babycakes was a lot more hammered than I had initially given him credit for.

He started slurring at this point, so I ordered a pizza. I hoped the addition of a greasy meal would save him from the inevitable hangover pain that daylight would bring. I practically had a PhD in Babycakes by this point and knowing what level of "Babycakes hammered" would equate to what level of "Babycakes hangover," I was scared.

When the pizza arrived, he was passed out on the couch. I roused him from his snoring and did my best to stuff him full of pie. By then his eyes were the color of a Bloody Mary and he wasn't interested in eating. He was referring to himself in the third person and had gone full-caveman.

"Babycakes. Sleep. Now," he grunted while I forced a greasy triangle into his maw.

I managed to stuff in two slices while encouraging him

to drink heavily from a bottle of Gatorade. He mostly resisted my efforts and trying to explain to him the benefits was futile.

I packed it in after this and helped Babycakes to bed. It was no small feat and required me to remove his suit—an expensive navy pinstripe that wrinkled easily—and shirt. When I finally let go of him, he fell to the bed with his arms outstretched, his mouth gaping in silent agony and his head lolled to one side. It was Renaissance-esque—a modern-day depiction of Rembrandt's *Jesus on the Cross*. There were small differences, of course: Jesus wore a loin cloth whereas Babycakes wore tighty-whities; instead of screaming, Babycakes was snoring. And he might die, yes, but only for his sin—of consumption.

Looking at him, like some sort of hangover oracle, I felt the urge to vomit. I was sure that he would be doing the same in several short hours.

I went to bed around 10 p.m. and woke up around 7:30 a.m. to the sound of a painful groaning. The hangover had arrived, right on cue. I glanced over and saw sweat rolling down Babycakes' head while the vein in his temple pulsed in sync with his dehydrated heart.

Why did I let him get that drunk, he questioned? I tried to explain to him my attempted pizza intervention, but he interrupted me for a more urgent matter. Babycakes, he announced, needed coffee, and Babycakes needed food. And if there was one thing that I knew about a hungover Babycakes, it was that the only sustenance that would suffice was a breakfast sandwich, hash-brown, and coffee from Tim Hortons. Fortunately for him, there was a Tim Hortons several short blocks away from my place—which is how Babycakes, sweating bullets through his designer suit, ended up vomiting outside of Tim Hortons at 8 a.m. on a Friday. Responsible adults walked past him on their way to work as he heaved and emptied the contents of his stomach onto the sidewalk.

There are several things that divide humans—wealth, country, and culture to name a few—but liquor really is the great equalizer. While Babycakes might have tens of millions of dollars and connections to some of the wealthiest and, arguably, most important people in North America, his inability to negotiate or pay his way out of a hangover marked him as merely another mortal among men.

SIX DEGREES OF A SERIAL KILLER

I was out with my cousin one evening at a storied dive bar. You know the kind—the bar is sticky, the drinks are cheap, and an aroma of stale beer permeates every inch of the inside. We ordered up a round of drinks—a vodka for my cousin, a beer for myself—and had just turned away from the bartender when a man in a crisp-white button-down shirt approached us. He was tall, around 6' 4", wore jeans, had close-cropped dirty-blond hair, and a confident air about him.

"Hi!" his big smile revealed a perfect set of pearly-whites.

We returned the greeting and he introduced himself as Terry.

"Jane," I stuck my hand out before my cousin introduced herself as well.

"Can I buy you two a drink?" he asked, gesturing to our clearly just-refreshed drinks. We demurred and Terry took the opportunity to talk about himself.

"I'm in lawn care," he said proudly and then droned on about his company. We listened politely, but Terry wasn't my type and I could see that my cousin's interest was waning. From the look on Terry's face, he could see this, too.

"That's great, good for you, Terry," my cousin said with more enthusiasm than the situation warranted. I knew what was coming from her next—a polite "It was great talking to you," before we moved on in search of someone more appealing.

"Hey!" Terry made a last-ditch attempt to reclaim our attention. "Do you guys know Paul Bernardo?"

My eyes went wide and I saw my expression mirrored by my cousin.

Paul Bernardo? Canada's most notorious serial killer? The man known as one half of the Barbie-and-Ken killers? The man who had brutally raped and killed three teenagers and who had picked up the name The Scarborough Rapist along the way?

Obviously we knew who he was. *Everyone* in Canada knew who he was.

"I know him," Terry said proudly. "His lawyer is my neighbour."

I was stunned.

Was this really what the dating pool had been reduced to? Things were so bad that men were relying on their six degrees of separation to serial killers?

My cousin and I quickly moved on and avoided Terry for the rest of the evening. I watched from afar as he approached women and struck out one by one. Then, twenty minutes before the bar closed, I spotted Terry near the exit. He was in the company of an attractive woman and he left with her shortly after.

I was surprised by this but I really shouldn't have been. I suppose it's not too much of a shock that someone would find Terry's proximity to "celebrity" appealing. The fact that it was his go-to pick-up line meant that he had likely used it before. And given his success/fail rate that evening, he didn't actually do too terribly. Twelve women's disgust is, apparently, one woman's delight.

THE DOUBLE DATE

I had a rule when I was dating Babycakes: I would go on double dates with potential clients only if he could guarantee that I would not be stuck making small talk with someone vapid. I realize that this makes me sound like a bitch and, while I definitely can be, my reasoning was that I only saw Babycakes for two three-day stints per month, and having to spend one of those nights in the company of a woman who has the conversation skills of Miss Teen USA, South Carolina, circa 2007, was exhausting.

This particular evening, Babycakes had promised me it wouldn't be that bad. We walked into the bar, grabbed a table, and waited for the potential client and his date.

Ten minutes later, Bruce, an attractive, gray-haired man walked in. Beside him was a girl in her early twenties who was wearing a sheer shirt with a black bra. And when I say "sheer shirt," I mean I've seen Saran Wrap that provided more coverage.

They took a seat, and the woman enthusiastically introduced herself.

"I'm Stephanie Jennifer!" she said, bouncing her curled brunette hair around.

She was bubbly, I'll give her that.

While Bruce and Babycakes started bullshitting, I turned to Stephanie Jennifer. She spoke like a Valley Girl, and I watched as the two brain cells she possessed fought it out for third place.

"You, like, totally, have to, like, *like* my fan page on Facebook," she enthused. "I'm, like, an actress and, like, a model."

I kicked Babycakes under the table but smiled at Stephanie Jennifer politely. She took this as a cue to tell me about her latest modeling job—a music video shoot where: "We, like, wore bikinis and, like, rode motorcycles to, like, a church, and then, like, we went inside and we partied. It was, like, so badass."

I kept smiling at her politely.

"You, like, have to come to the next music video shoot. They are, like, so fun."

The conversation between Stephanie Jennifer and I went on like this for the better part of an hour. When I told her that I worked at a lifestyle magazine she exclaimed, "Oh my god! I think I have that one!"—failing to understand that "lifestyle" was the genre and not the name of the publication itself.

It was painful, but at least there was liquor. And to that end, Stephanie Jennifer downed several drinks before we headed to our next location, which was another bar.

At the new place, we sat in a booth and ordered up tequila shots. Stephanie Jennifer enthusiastically chugged them down before we walked across the street to a karaoke bar. It wasn't one of those bars where there are separate rooms. It was an establishment with one stage that allowed everyone in the room to watch.

Stephanie Jennifer was seriously liquored up by that time and jumped at the chance to flex her vocal cords. She signed up for a few songs and we grabbed drinks while we waited for her turn. Because she was so drunk, she was being a bit obnoxious (who hasn't been there) and Bruce looked less than pleased.

Nonetheless, ten minutes later, Stephanie Jennifer took the stage. I assumed that she was good with her mouth and wondered if singing was one of her doubtlessly many talents. She was ambitious with her song choices, Carrie Underwood and Mariah Carey, two pop divas known for hitting the high notes. Stephanie Jennifer? Not so much.

I had been to this karaoke bar on several occasions and it was one of the most welcoming places I had ever been. The patrons were sweet and supportive, they clapped even if you were terribly off-key, and at the end of your song, everyone applauded. I am no vocalist myself, but I do like to sing. There have been some terrible soloists who have taken the stage, but the crowd always cheered.

Not so with Stephanie Jennifer.

It was the only time I had been in that bar where I witnessed patrons grimacing in pain; people were making hand-sandwiches with their heads. Stephanie Jennifer wasn't so much singing as she was screaming, off-key, into the microphone.

Babycakes and I sat there mesmerized while Bruce excused himself to go to the washroom.

He never came back.

When Stephanie Jennifer returned to our table, basking in the glow of being on stage, she looked around, confused. Where was Bruce?

I felt badly for her and gently let her know that Bruce had gone home.

Babycakes, owing to the massive amounts of vodka he

had ingested that evening, was feeling less than charitable towards her.

"You should go now," he told her. I saw tears well up in her eyes before she grabbed her purse and ran for the door.

I glared at Babycakes and went after her. Sure, I hadn't particularly liked her or enjoyed her company that evening, but I wasn't going to be cruel. When I caught up with her, I apologized for Babycakes' behavior and invited her to join us for a drink. She agreed.

Babycakes went to the bar while I consoled Stephanie Jennifer, who was now wailing dramatically and had tears streaming down her face. When Babycakes placed a vodka in front of her, she took a long drink, set down her glass, and wiped away her tears.

"I just wanted a sugar daddy," she cried, in what was an obvious reference to her date, Bruce.

I was surprised by this. I had assumed that she was dating Bruce for his money, but I had never before heard someone actually vocalize their material motives. And while her admission did not raise my opinion of her, the fact that she was being so honest about what she wanted did give me thismuch respect for her.

"Listen," I consoled her. "If that's what you want, Bruce is not the guy who you want to date." I then told her about a newly launched website that had come my way via my work email. It paired up sugar daddies with sugar babies, and they had contacted me in hopes of gaining media coverage. When I read the email I laughed and deleted it, but not before clicking on their site. If Stephanie Jennifer was looking for a sugar daddy, I suggested that maybe this website would be a good avenue.

"You're a bitch!" Stephanie Jennifer suddenly shouted at me.

I was confused.

"You're calling me a slut!" she yelled before grabbing her purse and legging it for the door.

"What the fuck did you say to her?" asked Babycakes, who had watched the whole thing go down.

I told Babycakes what had happened, and he agreed that I was being a bitch.

I was even more confused. I had genuinely been trying to help Stephanie Jennifer because I felt really awful for her. She was young, had gotten annihilated, her date had abandoned her, and she was just looking for someone to take care of her. For some reason, it had pulled at my heart strings. But in trying to be nice, I was perceived as a bitch. Which was odd, because when I was being a bitch to her earlier in the evening, she had thought that I was being nice. Akin to the "tree falling in the forest" query, it begged the question: if you're being a bitch to someone but they are too stupid to know it, are you really being mean?

I never saw Stephanie Jennifer again, but I have a sneaking suspicion that, during one of our many breakups, Babycakes took her out and banged her. Of course, he will never admit to it, but he has let enough slip during tipsy conversations that I would bet a large sum of money that it happened.

I did Google Stephanie Jennifer several years later out of morbid curiosity, and I discovered that she did eventually find her sugar daddy: a surgeon.

I am envious that she managed to find someone to settle down with, but I am also baffled by the fact that she settled down with a surgeon. I've dated several and mostly found them to be cold, unfeeling, and unaffectionate. But Stephanie Jennifer's bubbly persona clearly managed to melt one particular surgeon's heart. Although, I have seen several photos of her husband wearing a dress on different occasions, so it might actually be the case that he happily found someone who was cool with his cross-dressing.

Good for her.

MR. SITUATIONSHIP 3

I planned an early Christmas vacation one year and would be away for most of December. Brent and I wanted to see each other before I left, but we had a difficult time setting a date. He was busy. It was the Christmas season and come December 1st, if there was a party to attend, he would be there. Some people run marathons to test their strength, but for Brent, the holiday social circuit was his personal test of endurance. He prepared for it like a seasoned athlete and refrained from drinking for an entire month beforehand in anticipation of testing his liver's ability to process liquor. Some days, he had up to four social gatherings on his schedule: a three-hour Christmas brunch at Bymark followed by drinks at RBC, a holiday party hosted by investors, and a boozy dinner with friends that went until 1 a.m. In December, if he wasn't drunk, he was hungover. He had arrived on my doorstep one Sunday morning looking like a consumption-ravaged orphan from the Victorian era. I had never heard of anyone dying from a hangover before, but that morning, I would have put my money on Brent.

As a result of his social calendar and next-day sickness, it was hard to find a time for the two of us to get together, but after much back and forth, we made a date to meet for lunch two days before my flight. He was at his Etobicoke office that day, a good thirty-minute drive away, and he had a very tight schedule. He was going to beg off a team Christmas lunch, but he had to be back at the office by 1 p.m. Due to our small window of time, "lunch" somehow morphed into a last-minute hotel liaison with a bottle of wine. I turned on some music, placed a bottle of wine on the table, set out two glasses, and waited. Thirty minutes later, there was a knock at the door. I opened it and in walked Brent.

"Thanks for coming," I smiled, delighted that he had opted out of lunch with his business partners to see me.

He took a seat beside the couch and grinned at me: "I told my business partners that I had to meet with my portfolio manager."

I raised one of my eyebrows.

Portfolio manager?

I thought back to the times that he had said we couldn't get together because he had to meet with his portfolio manager. Oh god.

I grabbed a corkscrew and thrust it into the wine, cranking the screw with a lot more aggression than was warranted. An hour later, Brent, looking distinctly toasty, left, and I sat back and sipped the remainder of the wine. I had made no mention about the "portfolio manager" comment before he left, but I hadn't forgotten about it. I figured that we could have *that* talk after Christmas. Besides, even if we had *had* that talk, it was December and, therefore, unlikely that, come January, Brent would even remember.

When we met up in the New Year and Brent said that

he told his friends he had a commitment that evening (me) I gave him an ultimatum: in three months' time, I didn't want to be a portfolio manager, an event, or a commitment. I wanted to be a person.

As luck would have it, I was granted that status two months later. One of Brent's old work colleagues, Arthur, saw us in a restaurant and came by to say hi.

"Arthur, good to see you." Brent looked at his former colleague and then gestured towards me. "This is my friend, Jane."

Friend.

I had graduated from a fake finance professional, a party, and an obligation, but I wasn't sure if "friend" was any better. It was like going to the doctor and finding out that you have chlamydia, not cancer. It's not as bad as cancer, sure, but—the shame. Although, I had to admit that it was starting to feel like an adventure—nay, a challenge—what label would I progress to next? And what would I have to do to get there? The steps towards formally being recognized as Brent's girlfriend felt like running a multi-tour ultramarathon. There was pain, there was suffering, there was a strong desire to quit, and doubt over whether or not I could continue. But at the same time, there was an even stronger desire to push through it and secure a win. I pictured myself dragging my body through Death Valley at the tail end of a 765-day painful race. I willed myself to continue, seeing the finish line in sight. Standing there, next to the checkered line that indicated achievement, was Brent. Over the top of the finish line, above him, hung a banner that read: "Special Friend." I wasn't even sure that I *liked* Brent at this point, but when it came to winning, you could count me in.

BABYCAKES 21

We were having cocktails at a hotel bar one evening when Babycakes and I began reminiscing about our long and storied relationship.

"You know," he sat back, looking pensive, "you're more attractive now than the day I met you."

I was flattered. After all, I had aged many years (twelve to be exact) since we met and, despite my best efforts, I was not aging like a fine wine. Several times I had found myself gently stroking the petal-soft skin of a baby while bemoaning the fact that my skin did not feel the same. *"I want his skin!"* I had moaned at my three-month-old nephew like I was a more-monstrous version of Cruella de Vil. My sister had looked at me sideways: *"Okay there, Buffalo Bill. Stay away from my baby."*

"You have more confidence," Babycakes said, taking a sip of his drink. "It's attractive."

"Thanks, Babycakes." A happy smile spread across my face.

He continued: "I mean, I don't need to be with an eleven."

I paused. So, I was attractive but I wasn't *that* attractive. And the conviction with which Babycakes had said it made it clear that he was being sincere. I actually think he thought he was giving me a compliment.

A frown that started at my eyes and reached all of the way down quickly replaced my smile. I wasn't an eleven on the 1-to-10 scale, and now my grimace would probably qualify me as the Grinch.

Now, don't get me wrong. I don't think for a second that I am the hottest woman on the planet—not even close. But the last thing I want from my partner is for him to tell me that I'm attractive and then add a caveat lest I get the wrong impression that I could be a cover girl. That was going to be my fun "About Me" fact from now on any time I was thrust into one of those ice-breaker conversations. "Hi, I'm Jane. And a fun fact about me is that I am not an 11."

Babycakes saw my frown and fully realized what he had said.

"I've never seen an eleven," he fumbled, trying in vain to recover. "And your personality makes you a twelve."

We were bringing personalities into it now. Miss Congeniality was rearing her ugly head. It reminded me of the time that I had excitedly sent a girlfriend a photo of the new man I was dating. Two minutes passed before a message popped up on my screen: *He has kind eyes,* it said.

I almost dumped him right then and there. The most attractive photo I could find of him hadn't even elicited the standard *He's cute!* line that's used any time a friend is dating a man who is anything but.

Kind eyes.

That was me.

Spoken by the man who I had dated on-and-off for the better part of a decade.

THE BILL

I met Tyler on multiple occasions through mutual friends. He was handsome, sixteen years my senior, successful in sales, and seemed to always be at the bar. He was also perpetually single and known to be a bit of a playboy. We bantered back and forth at a ritzy private club one evening and exchanged numbers. The night culminated in Tyler being escorted out of the venue by several staffers. Previous group outings had alerted me to the fact that when he drank white wine, he turned into an asshole. White wine, I later discovered, was Tyler's drink of choice. Which meant that he was an asshole a lot and that he had been kicked out of too many bars to count. Nevertheless, we messaged each other a few days later and made plans for a Thursday night. He lived in the entertainment district and we agreed to go to a restaurant in his building.

It was a warm summer night and I wore stilettos and a mini-dress; Tyler wore loafers, white jeans, and a smart shirt. We had one drink at the restaurant before Tyler realized he had left his wallet upstairs.

"Do you mind coming up while I grab it?" he asked after fishing $20 out of his pocket and throwing it on the table.

I didn't mind and I also didn't think that it was a ploy to get me into bed. I had seen the mix of panic and surprise on his face when he realized he didn't have his wallet. Once upstairs we shared a bottle of wine while deciding where to go. Eventually, we settled on hitting up a tiki bar and headed out for the night.

Hidden on the roof of a grungy dive bar, the tiki bar was located up two sets of stairs and was entirely outside. The bar sat on one end and offered up fruity drinks served in pineapples and standard libations. Eclectic music blasted through the speakers and picnic tables dotted the small space.

Tyler immediately opened up a tab and ordered us drinks. Beer for me, vodka for him. We sat at one of the picnic tables, drank, and chatted into the evening. More people piled into the bar as the sky began to darken and soon the place was packed.

I was three drinks deep when Tyler suggested that we do shots, which we did with unbridled enthusiasm. Tyler's enthusiasm was such that he began buying shots for the people standing around us at the bar. Vodka, tequila, more vodka, more tequila. It was a jovial scene—people laughing and clinking shot glasses in celebration of free liquor. Tyler continued to buy shots for strangers over the next few hours.

Around midnight I felt the urge to dance on a table. Tyler, more than willing to accommodate, helped me up and soon other patrons began to follow. My stiletto got stuck in the crack between the table slats and Tyler helped me down shortly after. Then we kissed, drank, and kissed some more until last call.

I nursed my drink while Tyler went to settle up the bar tab but after five minutes of waiting, I waded through the crowd towards him. He was standing there in, what looked like, a serious conversation with the bartender. I asked if everything was okay. The bartender looked annoyed.

"His card was declined."

I glanced at Tyler.

"How much is the bill?"

The bartender handed me a receipt and I did a double take. Tyler, mostly due to his liberal shot buying for strangers, had amassed a bar tab that was more than $350.

The bartender and Tyler both looked at me expectantly. I didn't know what to do. I didn't particularly want to pay the bill, but if I didn't, would the police come and ticket Tyler? Would he be charged with something or arrested? Neither Tyler nor the bartender offered up any alternatives and I hesitated before pulling out my debit card and paying the exorbitant amount. I was a university student at the time and $350 would normally cover the cost of my groceries for an entire month. Instead, I was throwing a month's worth of grocery money away to avoid having my date reap the consequences of his own actions.

We got into a taxi shortly after that and I gave the address to my place. The car ride was mostly silent—the jovial mood of twenty minutes before had soured. I had no problem paying for our drinks. But I did have a problem paying for the forty-some shots he had purchased for other people.

"I'll e-transfer you the money tomorrow," Tyler promised.

I looked at him and said nothing.

When the car pulled up to my building, Tyler turned to me expectantly: "So, what's the deal? Am I coming up?"

I could scarcely believe him. He had stuck me with a $350 bar tab without so much as an apology and was expecting to get laid on our first date. "No, you're not coming up."

"Fine, suit yourself," he said rudely as I exited the vehicle. He hadn't drank white wine that night, but I surmised that vodka must turn him into a dick, too.

I went to bed alone that evening with my bank account $350 lighter. Tyler never did repay me. Not that I'm keeping track or anything.

BABYCAKES 22

In an earlier chapter, I wrote about the night I thought Babycakes was going to propose and the relief I felt upon seeing that the velvet box contained a necklace and not a ring. Fast forward several years, and I did finally receive a proposal from Babycakes. Sort of.

He claimed that it was a proposal, while I maintained that it was a preface. And what exactly did this proposal/preface consist of? Let me set the scene.

I had finally gotten fed up and accepted the fact that our relationship was going nowhere. It had only taken me eight years to arrive at this conclusion, but in the game of love, I am slower than the second coming of Christ.

Babycakes was never going to take me to his city and introduce me to his friends and family; he was never going to move here or allow me to move there; he would never integrate me into his life in any kind of meaningful way. There was no viable future for us. Upon reaching that conclusion, I signed up for some dating apps. I met a few men whom I clicked with and started going out on dates. One man I got along with very well, and things between us seemed to be headed in a promising direction. We hadn't discussed exclusivity, and he lived on the other side of the world, but he was coming back on an extended stay for business and to see me. This trip, however, was two months away, and in a bit of a coincidence, I ended up in Babycakes' city that summer.

I let him know I was in town and that I hoped we could spend some time together. I still loved him, even though we had broken up, and relationship-wise, I knew that we would never be anything more than lovers and sometimes friends. But I accepted it. Resentment, anger, and hostility can be exhausting, and they are feelings that I had clung to for far too long.

There is something so liberating about finally letting go and accepting things for what they are and for what they never will be. I had accepted a long time ago that Babycakes would never be sober, but accepting the reality that our relationship wasn't going anywhere had taken me a lot longer. My hope had been like the eternal flame on one of those magic candles—it refused to die. Just when you think you've blown it out, it would spark back to life in a flicker of orange and yellow: the "little candle that could." And in the end, I don't think that the flame was even extinguished by the gale-force winds of our dysfunction. I think it just reached the end of its wick, and there was nothing left to fuel the fire.

When I contacted Babycakes, he was initially reluctant to meet me. He didn't want to rehash old fights and was concerned that I was still pining for him. After a few back-and-forth texts, he begrudgingly agreed to get together. For dinner, we went to a Michelin star restaurant at the top of a tall building. Aside from four other patrons, we were the only people there. I am convinced that Babycakes chose this place because he figured that no one he knew would see him there. And, more importantly, no one he knew would see him there with me.

Despite Babycakes' initial reluctance, he was having a good time. Maybe it was because we weren't fighting, which had been a hallmark of our time together for the past couple of years. I took responsibility for most of it, given that my frustration with the state of our relationship had been the source of most of our warring. But my newfound acceptance had freed me. No longer did I feel frustrated, upset, angry, or annoyed. I felt lighter, and it really allowed me to be myself and have fun with Babycakes like we used to.

We were halfway through our meal when he asked me how things were back home.

"I met someone," I told him.

Babycakes suddenly looked crestfallen. I found this confusing, as I thought he would be happy for me. After all, he had made it perfectly clear that nothing more would ever happen between us. If I wanted to be with him, I had to be happy spending the next forty years of my life living in a different city without knowing his friends and family. Essentially, a long-distance mistress.

He hadn't even wanted to see me that night.

But I had forgotten about Babycakes' competitiveness—something that had made him such a success in the cutthroat world of finance. Me, sad, resentful, frustrated, and pining for Babycakes, was a turn-off. Me, happy, carefree, fun, and interested in someone else, was a turn-on. And suddenly, Babycakes was all in.

We spent an enjoyable evening together and the next two months—before my international paramour was slated to arrive—consisted of Babycakes trying his hardest to win me back.

Now, had my candle not reached the end of its wick, I

probably would have fallen for it. After all, I loved Babycakes and had spent several years hoping for this very thing. But the new me, the one without a wick, was not going to buy Babycakes' bullshit. If he wanted to win me back, I told him, I wanted a condo and a ring. When it came to Babycakes, words were worthless. But money? That talked.

Six days before my international man was scheduled to arrive, a desperate Babycakes called me. While he had been doing his very best to win me back by sending me near-daily bouquets of flowers, being attentive, and coming to see me, he hadn't met my terms and conditions. I had no ring, and I had no condo.

"Listen," he said to me on the phone one night, desperation creeping into his voice. "What would you say if I asked you to marry me?"

I was dumbfounded for two reasons:

1. It sounded like Babycakes was wading into marriage territory. We were broaching a great unknown, and it didn't so much seem like it was coming from the heart as it was from some deep-seated need to win a rivalry that the other man didn't even know he was embroiled in.

2. He wasn't outright proposing to me. No, no. He was gauging what my interest was and what my response would be. Babycakes was hedging his bet when it came to asking for my hand in marriage.

All I could picture was Jim Carey in *Dumb and Dumber*:

"What do you think the chances are of a guy like you and a girl like me ending up together?" Carey asks Mary.

"Not good," Mary replies.

"Not good like one in a hundred?" he asks.

She looks at him pitifully: *"I'd say more like one in a million."*

A slow smile spreads across Carey's face: *"So you're telling me there's a chance."*

Somehow, I sensed that Babycakes wouldn't pull the trigger unless the odds were more fully in his favor.

In my case, I didn't know what to say. And I didn't know what I *would* say if Babycakes asked me to marry him. All *I* knew was that, if that was what he considered to be a marriage proposal, it needed work.

"I don't know what I would say," I replied, my eyebrows scrunched in confusion. "If you want an answer, ask me the fucking question, and propose with the fucking ring."

Babycakes deferred and, in reference to a man who was mentioned earlier in this book ("The Dearly Deported"), before I was able to see my international paramour, he was deported.

When Babycakes found out, he looked like he had won the lottery. His competition had literally disappeared overnight on a trans-Pacific flight. And he was now off the hook when it came to giving me a condo and a ring. There is no winning when the tournament consists of one team. I was a participation trophy at this point.

As I had anticipated, in the absence of competition, Babycakes dropped all ideas of marriage and a shared condo in my city. According to him, I had actually turned down his telephone marriage proposal. I had crushed him when I told him that I didn't know what I would say if he proposed to me, so he couldn't possibly be expected to want to seriously date me now.

I wish I could say that I stayed in my Zen state of acceptance, where I apathetically received anything that came my way. And I could, but it would be a lie.

Instead, I spent the next several months in a state of devastation. I had picked out a ring, and I had been hopeful. If Babycakes didn't propose, at least I was secure in knowing that I was starting something new with a man whom I loved spending time with, who was interested in me, and who treated me well. Instead, I wound up with nothing and no one.

I lost 10lbs due to stress and gained a new appreciation for dark humor. But I didn't wallow. Why wallow, when you can wine?

MR. SITUATIONSHIP 4

One Thursday evening, Brent and I met for dinner. I wasn't aware that he had spent all afternoon drinking and only realized this when I showed up at the steakhouse. His eyes were red-rimmed and glassy and he had a haughty air about him.

"Business meetings," he grunted before ordering up a nine-ounce glass of wine.

I grimaced as the bartender placed a twelve-ounce glass in front of him.

Fantastic. He would be slurring by 7 p.m.

He asked me the name of our bartender, who we were friendly with and who had served us on several occasions, but I couldn't recall. Brent berated me for it.

"You should remember!" he said aggressively. This was in spite of the fact that he was unable to remember the bartender's name himself. He kept notes in his phone that included people's names, places of work, and short descriptions of what they looked like—a move that ensured waitstaff saw him as genial and genuine even though it was contrived. He had forgotten to type out the details of this one particular bartender, and me not being able to tell him who the bartender was reflected poorly on Brent.

"Not knowing his name looks bad," Brent said fiercely.

I rolled my eyes and said nothing. He was a 6' 2" human wine bottle at this point and I had never gotten into an argument with a bottle of wine and won.

He continued being unpleasant for most of the evening, and only turned jocular during the walk home. During dinner, he ordered up more alcohol and by the time we left the restaurant, he was blasted. It was a slow walk back to my place as I tried to keep him in check—he laughed, pinched my behind, put his hand up my skirt, and stumbled over the uneven sidewalk. At one point, he stepped in front of oncoming traffic and I had to drag him back to safety. Autopilot Brent was a danger to himself and those around him.

Halfway back to my condo, I stepped in a sidewalk crack and one of my shoes became stuck. Brent, blissfully unaware of much of anything, kept marching forward as I tried to free my foot. It took a minute, but I managed to dislodge my high heel and caught up to Brent who was leading the way back to my place like the exuberant Grand Marshal of a Thanksgiving Day parade. He hadn't even realized that I was missing.

When we made it back to my condo, we quickly got down to business. Afterward, we lay there together and I snuggled up next to him. His eyes were closed and I traced my fingers along his chest as his breathing took on a deeper, more relaxed tempo.

"I bought some outfits," I said after a couple of minutes. "Do you want me to send you sexy photos?"

Brent, his eyes still closed, didn't miss a beat: "No, thanks," he said. "Give Brent-o five minutes with no talking."

Give Brent-o five minutes with no talking?

What I *wanted* to do was tell Brent-o to go fuck himself—I had dealt with his drunken antics and snarky attitude towards me all night—but I did as he requested. He was so hammered that he likely wouldn't remember his behavior. Not that I was excusing it. He slipped into a snoring state minutes later and I lay there next to him, wondering just how hungover he was going to be the next day.

As it turned out, the answer was very. I texted him at work the following morning and he confirmed that he was, indeed, massively hungover. Did he remember what he had said to me the night before in bed when I asked if he wanted me to send him sexy photos? I questioned.

No, what? he replied.

You said "no thanks" followed by "Give Brent-o five minutes with no talking."

I received a rolling-on-the-floor-laughing emoji in reply.

Whatever, I mused. Brent was currently ensconced in Dante's sixth circle of hangover hell. It didn't exactly count as karmic retribution, but it felt like punishment enough.

THE INVESTMENT BANKER

Angus was an atypical banker. He was sober, vegan, and tattooed; a finance guy with Irish roots and a desire to travel and live in a van. He seemed kind, down-to-earth, and respectful—qualities that flew in the face of his career. Most bankers who I have met have been alcohol- or cocaine-abusing womanizers who work hard and party even harder.

We met on a dating app and went out a few times for drinks. On our third date we hit up a watering hole near my condo. Angus ordered a ginger beer and we got to chatting. I was curious about his sobriety but hadn't asked him about it. *None of my business,* I thought. If he wanted to tell me about it, he would. That night, he did.

In his younger years (he was in his mid-30s when we met) Angus explained that he had dabbled in every kind of hedonistic self-indulgence he could find. He drank to excess, used drugs to excess, and slept with women to excess. Eventually he realized that his hedonistic lifestyle wasn't serving him well. Some of the situations he had gotten himself into during that time were nauseating. But I didn't hold his past actions against him; he was sober now and it sounded like most of the damage that had been done was to himself. At least, that was my belief until he told me about a long-term relationship he had had during his mid-twenties. He had been dating a woman for six months but had decided that he didn't want to date her anymore. But instead of doing the mature thing and having a conversation with the woman, what did Angus do?

"I went and hooked up with a set of twins, recorded us having sex and sent the video to my girlfriend."

There was an unmistakable tinge of pride in his voice.

I was appalled, which was apparent, and Angus suddenly looked a bit abashed.

"Obviously I regret it now and I know how shitty it is," he said. "I wouldn't do that today."

For me, the damage was done. I can agree that it's unfair to judge someone for their past, but there are also some things that a person just can't get past.

There are also some things that are better left unsaid.

Unfortunately for me, I've said it all.

EPILOGUE

At the time of publication, I am still single. I still see Babycakes and we have settled into a friendly, drama-free routine. My last bad date was owing to Brent (a.k.a. Mr. Situationship). I've given up online dating and I am hoping that the next decade of my life will not end up as *50 Worst Dates: Part Two.*

ACKNOWLEDGEMENTS

Aside from the men who have made this book possible, there are several people without whom this project would never have gotten off the ground. Maggie, for prodding me to keep writing even when I didn't want to and for giving me feedback on each and every chapter—good and bad. Also, for keeping me in some form of sane during my spirals. Mom, Dad, and Trevor, for listening to my tipsy excerpts and laughing at the appropriate times. Babycakes—who I read his chapters to and who laughed out loud. (I didn't use your real name so you don't have to kill me.) "Brent" F.—for being a source of both inspiration and exasperation. Just give in already. Kimberley S., for finding the material funny and encouraging me to keep writing. Our phone calls and dinner dates are a never-ending source of joy and laughter. Tim "Hollywood" K., for singing praises about my writing to anyone who will listen—I so appreciate having you in my corner. Lastly, Carlin K., for providing me with endless hours of entertainment and emotional support.

ABOUT THE AUTHOR

Jane is an Indigenous writer who lives in Toronto, Canada. She writes rom-coms, chick-lit, and satire, and often draws from experiences in her own life.

In addition to writing, Jane is a wine and fashion enthusiast. She enjoys volunteering and supports several animal rescues.

Printed in the USA
CPSIA information can be obtained
at www.ICGtesting.com
LVHW031736261123
764944LV00004B/409

9 781739 049102

Made in the USA
Coppell, TX
06 June 2020

27130798R10236